AF231253

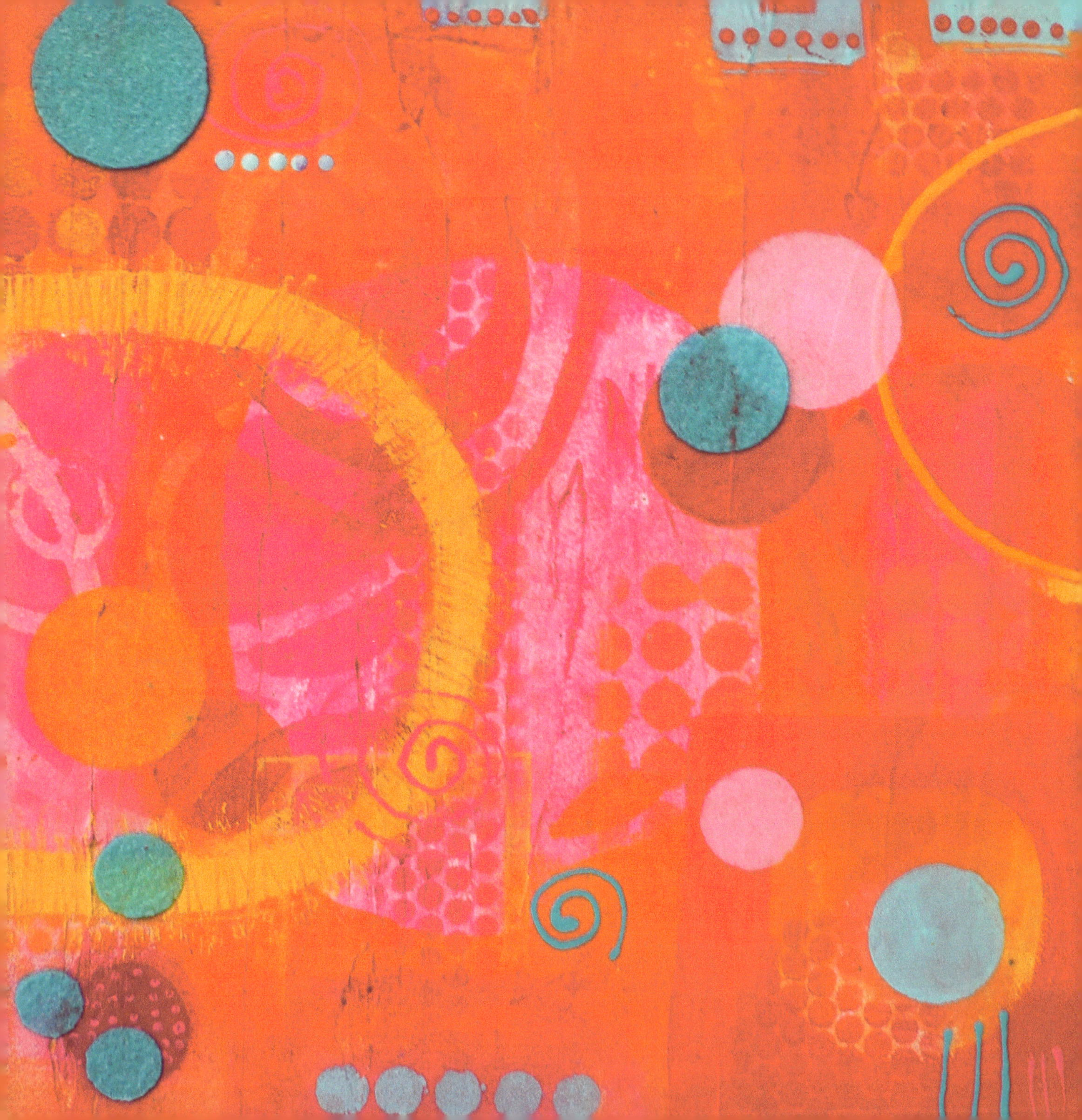

IT'S ONLY PAINTING

ESSAYS ON CREATIVITY
FROM A
VETERAN ARTIST

Tesia Blackburn

Also by Tesia Blackburn

"Acrylic Painting With Passion:
Explorations For Creating Art That Nourishes the Soul"

ISBN 978-0-692-17663-4

Design by Tesia Blackburn and Vanzzsolutions.com
Edited by Patrice Drago

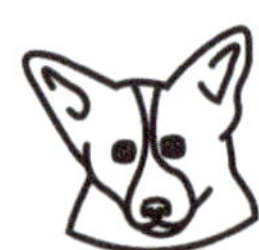

Team Soxx Publishing
PO Box 2023
South San Francisco, CA 94083

Printed in the United States of America

First printing October 2018

For my mom

""THE AIM OF ART IS TO REPRESENT NOT THE OUTWARD APPEARANCE OF THINGS, BUT THEIR INWARD SIGNIFICANCE."

Aristotle

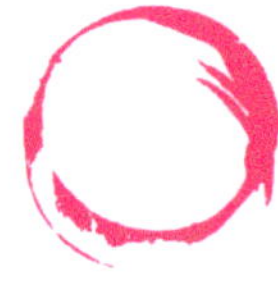

Table of Contents

Acknowledgements

Many thanks to these brave souls for purchasing an advance copy
of this book, sight unseen. My heartfelt thanks to all of you!

Ellen Abels • Jennifer Aceves • Lori Anderson •Bonnie Armstrong
• Carol Bear • Caroline Bengtson • Gordon Bruning • Karen
Buttwinick • Jackie Carroll • Sharon Cleary • Joyce Costa • Laura
Croyle • Celia Cuasay • Carol Doney • Norma Fowler • Simcha
Freedman • Terry Gartshore • Lynn Glenn • Gina Greisinger •
Suzette Hodnett • Sarah Horton • Terri Ingham • Susan Johnson •
Elaine Larson • Catherine Lecce-Chong • Laura Lush • Veronica
Madrid • Elise Marshall • Debra Martin • Patricia L McCarty •
Yolanda Mihic • Judy Miller • Nancy Morey • Sarah Morrison •
Lynda Newell • Peg OMalley • Gloria Orme • Barbara Rebhan
• Louise Reingold • Lynne Sonenberg • Susan St. Thomas • Lisa
Steele • Kandi Taylor • Alayne H. Trachewsky • Wendy Trotter
Alana Unger • Anni Weston

ACKNOWLEDGEMENTS

No book like this is written without the help of many people. My heartfelt thanks goes out to everyone who reviewed an early copy, my students who have heard these words over and over (and still listen) and to the many artists and teachers who I cross paths with and who inspire me daily, especially the generous Contributors to this book.

My amazing editor, Patrice Drago, is an angel beyond compare. Erudite and always on point, she kept me on task and never let me get away with anything!

I'm eternally grateful to B. for keeping the home fires burning and shoving a sandwich at me occasionally.

Finally, thanks Mom, wherever you are, for always believing in me.

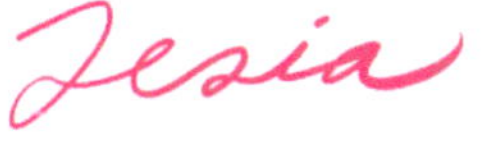

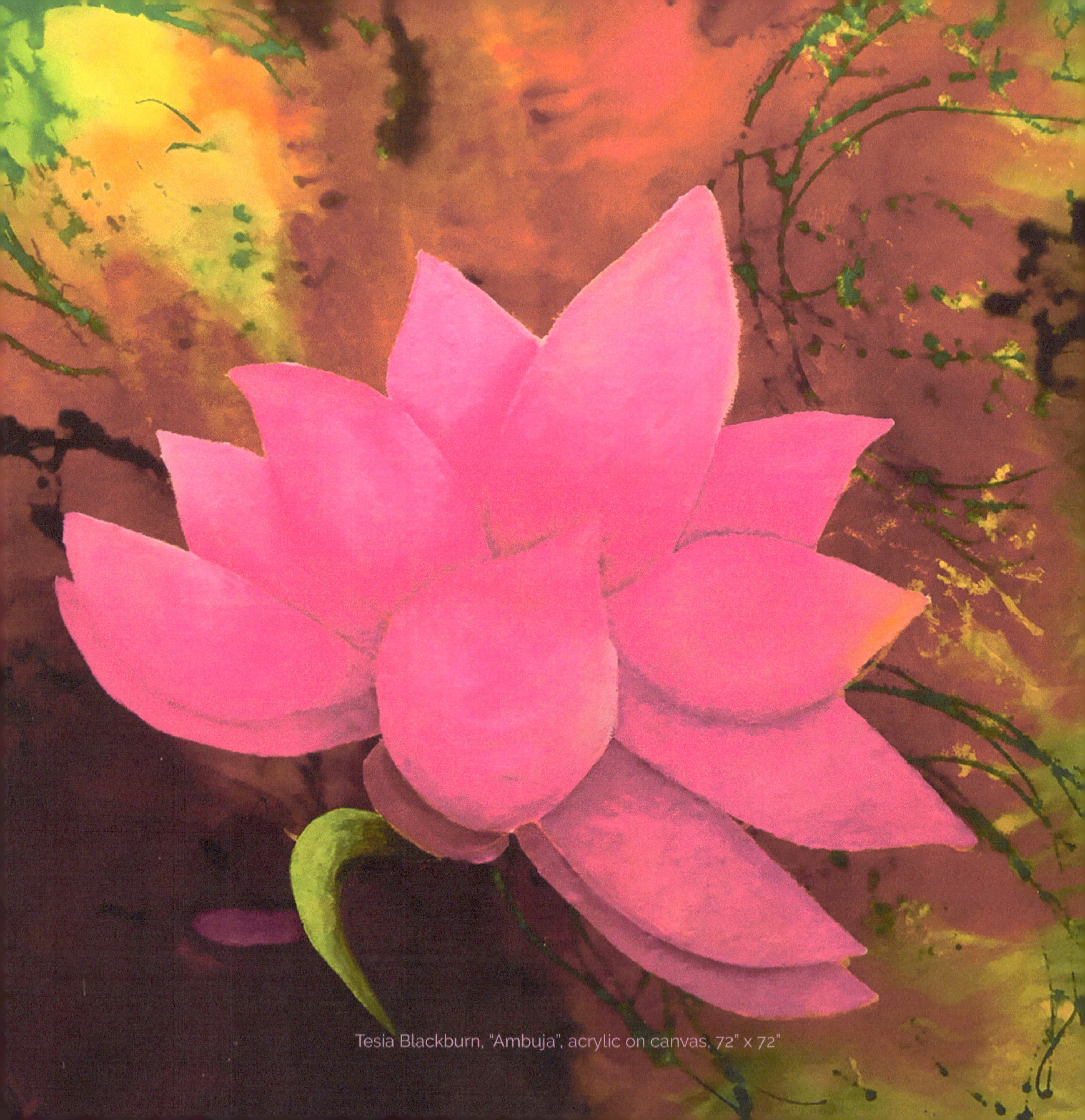

Tesia Blackburn, "Ambuja", acrylic on canvas, 72" x 72"

I'm glad you're here. I hope you'll read this book for what it is - me talking to you just like I've been talking to my students for the past 25 years or so.

I don't claim to have any miraculous insight into creativity. Just years and years of working with people who wonder the same things I do:

What is this creativity stuff?

How do I get started (or restarted) making art?

Where are my house keys?

Yeah, I can be silly. But I think that might be the key to making art of any kind. Don't take yourself too seriously. Just relax, make stuff and have fun.

Inside you'll notice sentence fragments, adult language, grammatical errors and even some contradictions. I write just like I talk. So grab a cup of coffee and hang out with me a little. I may just have a surprise or two for you.

With Love,

Jesia

"CREATIVITY IS MORE THAN JUST BEING DIFFERENT. ANYBODY CAN PLAN WEIRD; THAT'S EASY. WHAT'S HARD IS TO BE AS SIMPLE AS BACH. MAKING THE SIMPLE, AWESOMELY SIMPLE, THAT'S CREATIVITY."

Charles Mingus

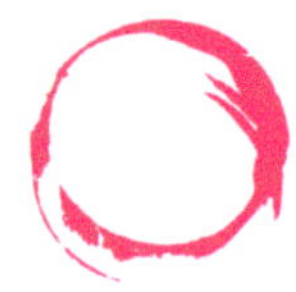

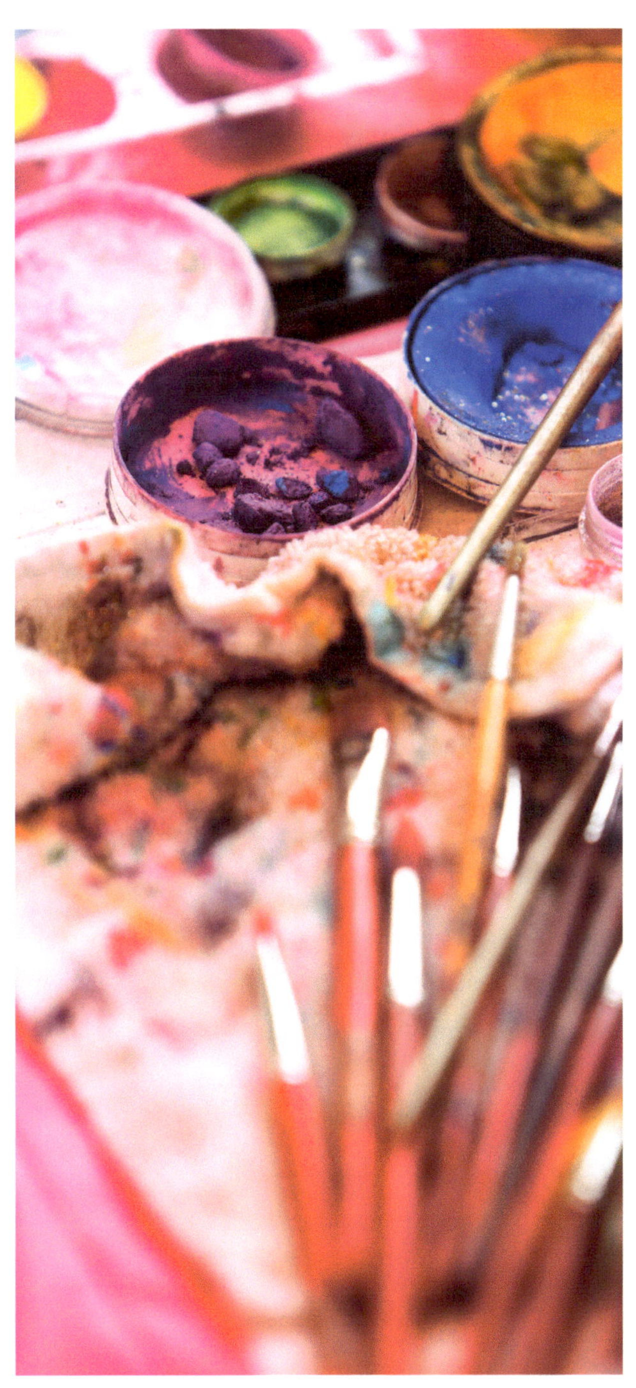

CHAPTER ONE

IT'S ONLY PAINTING

YOU should make stuff.

It doesn't matter if it's big or small. It doesn't matter if it's meant to last or to disappear. You should make stuff. You can make it with cotton swabs, tissue paper and string that you found in the trash. Or you can make it with the most archival professional grade artist materials available. Just don't be afraid to make stuff. Don't worry if it's any good. Just make it.

That's what I'm hoping you'll take away from this little book. I want to clear the way for you to make stuff. I want you to be inspired. I want it to be easy. I want you to make stuff even if you're afraid of it being no good, even if you don't know why you're making it. If you have a passion to create, you should create.

Some people have a passion to cook, some people garden or nurture children, some people sew. Me? I'm a maker. I make stuff. Mostly paintings and drawings but sometimes I make sculpture and sometimes I make things that aren't easily defined.

"Art is theft."
Picasso

Listen, I know there's already a lot of stuff in the world. But if you are called to make things, if your passion tells you that you should make things, then you should make them. You can make them so that they disappear. You can make them out of things that don't impact the earth like twigs, dirt, rocks and tree branches. The well-known British artist Andy Goldsworthy works with twigs, trees, flower petals and even icicles. His work is meant to eventually return to nature.

So go ahead, make that thing you've been thinking about. Make ten of them. Don't worry about whether you're really an artist, don't wait for divine inspiration. Just make stuff and enjoy your creativity.

Have fun.

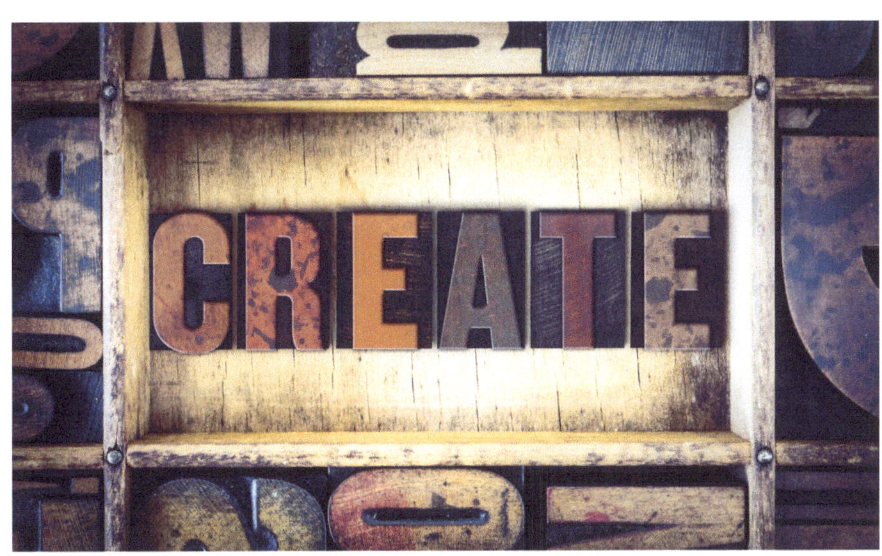

The biggest question you can ask yourself, and probably the most important, is what inspires me? Find something or someone that inspires you and start there. Chances are good that if you are inspired, your painting will have more life to it. This doesn't have to be a grandiose idea. As a matter of fact, those big ideas will probably get you into more trouble if you're just starting out. Save the Big Idea for later. To start, just work with something you find interesting. Maybe your son has a red bicycle that he loves. Well, that gives you two things, circles (tires) and color (red). That's plenty to get started on a series of paintings about your son's bicycle. Picasso broke open the entire modern era in art by creating a sculpture of a bull's head made from a bicycle seat and handlebars.

Never underestimate the power of the humble everyday object.

Look at the work of Marcel Duchamp and Joseph Cornell. Powerful work created with everyday objects.

Most of all keep a sense of humor about all of this creativity stuff. Remember, it's not brain surgery. If you make something lousy, no one will die.

It's only painting.

"Art is the only way to run away without leaving home."
Twyla Tharp

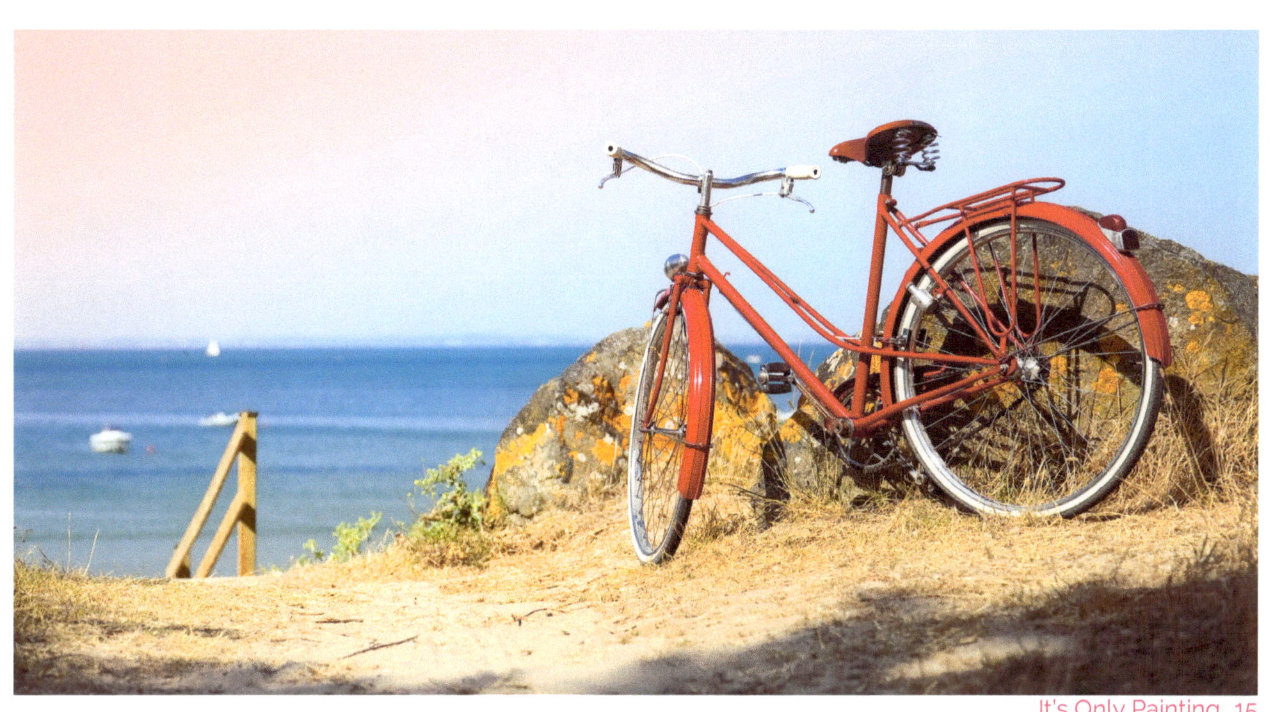

"Don't think. Thinking is the enemy of creativity. It's self-conscious, and anything self-conscious is lousy. You can't try to do things. You simply must do things."

Ray Bradbury

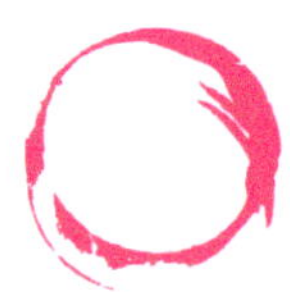

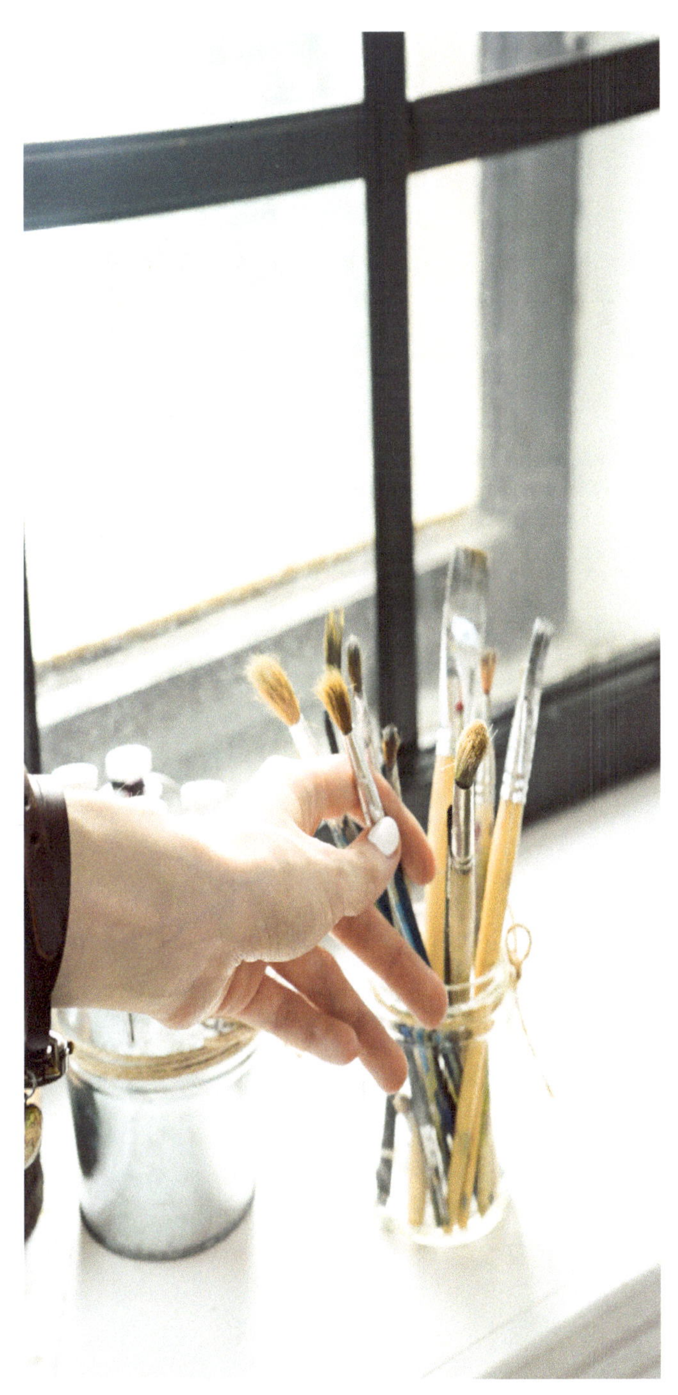

Chapter Two

The Myth of The Artist

Or

How Hollywood Kills Creativity

YOU know how when you're in the shower singing, and you're fabulous? Making art is like singing in the shower. If you create something and you love it, you think it's fabulous, guess what?

You're an artist.

Now I can hear you saying, "yes but I don't have any training" or "I don't know what I'm doing" or "how can everyone be an Artist?" Well the truth is, everyone IS an Artist. We just have to suppress it most of the time. We have to drive cars and make dinner and pick up the kids from school and go to jobs. But if we look back

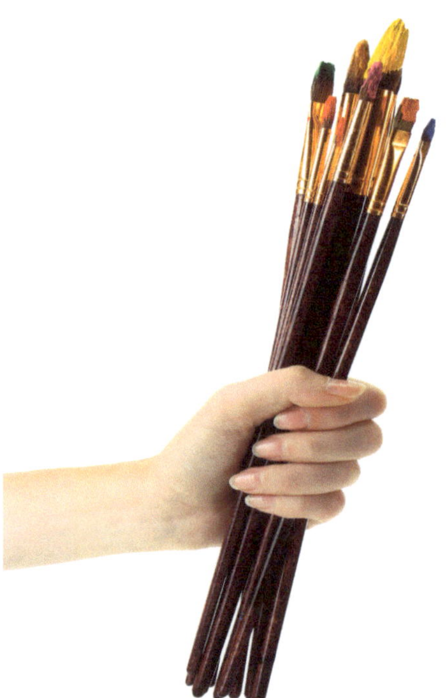

far enough, being an artist wasn't a specialized skill that only a few people had. Every member of the tribe could draw something on the wall of the cave or in the dirt around the fire. And if you ask any four year old to draw something for you, they will do it easily, without worrying if they're an "Artist" because they know they are. The idea of a being an Artist (with a capital A) is a relatively new idea. Up until the Renaissance, artists were just guild members doing their job for the Church or a wealthy patron. We don't even know most of their names prior to the Renaissance.

Then along came Leonardo da Vinci and Michelangelo Buonarotti, the first two Artist Superstars.

These guys were game changers, and the world of being an artist has never been the same. Fast forward to the 20th century, somewhere up to and including the days of Jackson Pollock, and the term artist took on a whole new meaning, surrounded by hype and stellar multi-million dollar deals.

But back before all of that, there was the artist. He – or she – worked every day perfecting their craft, diligently using the design tools we still use today. There's something awe-inspiring about this long line of artists we come from. With the same simple tools, they created art that we look at today with amazement. Some of it moves me to tears. And I don't even know their names.

So how do you reclaim the Artist inside you?

Like the ad says - just do it.

Sounds easy, right? You know it's not. I know it's not. That's why I wrote this book. Claiming your artistic soul is kind of like going on a diet. You just have to keep taking it a day at a time and avoid the donuts. Sigh. Donuts.

But what does that really look like?

Well first we have to dispel some myths around what it means to be an artist.

MYTH #1 - I should have an MFA or years and years of training to be an Artist.

Nothing could be further from the truth. And believe me, years of training (which I have) can sometimes get in the way of real creativity. It took me years to find my own voice after hearing my teachers in my head. Some of the world's best-known artists were self-taught. Perhaps you've heard of Vincent van Gogh? In my humble opinion, and the opinion of a lot of my students and peers, authenticity counts for a lot more than training. If you have something inside you that wants to be expressed, and you bring it to light, that's good enough for me. And it should be good enough for you, too. I could create a very long list of self-taught artists that didn't let the lack of a formal education deter them. It shouldn't deter you either.

This myth reminds me of the story I heard about the 50-year-old woman who wanted to start medical school. She was told she'd be nearly 60 when she graduated. Her answer? "Well I'm going to be 60 anyway. I might as well be a doctor!" It's never too late. Grandma Moses didn't start painting until she was 80. Emily Kngwarreye, an Australian Aboriginal painter, also didn't start painting until she was nearly 80. Both of these women have had major museum shows and passionate collectors.

So it's never too late.

And by the way, your life experience counts for a lot more than you realize. See the chapter "The School of Life."

"I was too old for a paper route, too young for Social Security and too tired for an affair."
Erma Bombeck

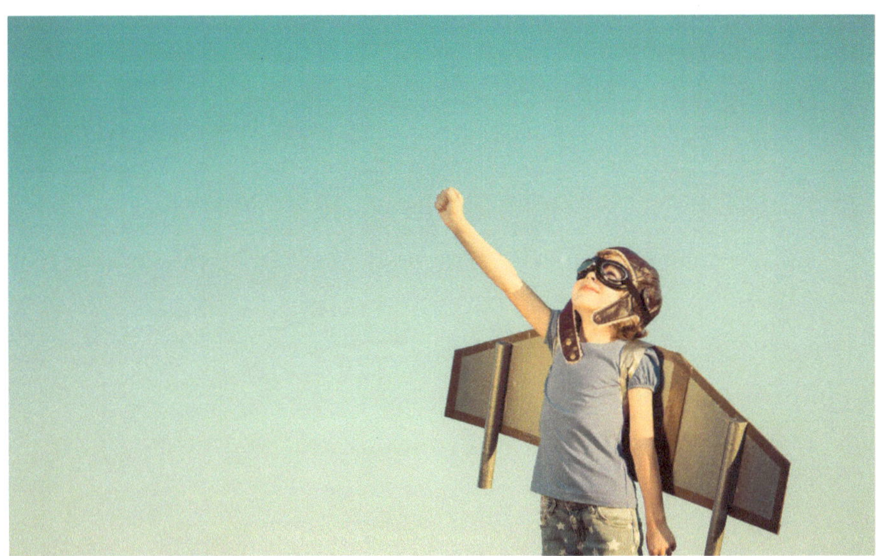

You think you're too young? You're not. I have been moved to tears by beginning students far younger than me. Their honesty and courage is refreshing. Their willingness to explore is a pleasure to watch. And when I get to witness one of their aha moments… well, just bring me a tissue because my old experienced artist heart has just cracked wide open.

See, if you're a youngster or a beginner, there's something you don't know. Experienced artists and teachers like myself have long since lost touch with those first, falling-in-love moments of creativity. Sure, I get those gooseflesh moments in the studio. But if I'm honest, there isn't much that happens on a canvas that surprises me. I'm an old pro at this, a journeyman, if you will. I get up and do my work every day and I am thankful for the moments of sheer bliss that surround me when I work. But surprises? Not many. Now don't get me wrong. I am continually exploring and pushing in my work. But paint on canvas only has so many permutations. Witnessing a brand new painter discovering her soul on the canvas is a whole other level of bliss.

So don't think that you are too young or too old to start.

Just start.

Right here, right now.

MYTH #3 - I need a 1,000-square-foot studio.

Here's another myth that needs to get kicked to the curb. I know many artists who work in the spare bedroom or in the garage. And if you're working small it doesn't take much time to make good stuff, because you can make a lot of it. The more you make, the better you get. It's that's simple. So unless you're going to start painting eight foot canvases, you can get a lot of work done between stirring the soup and folding the laundry. Right there on the corner of the kitchen table.

And you should.

Pranayama Series

The California artist Tina Pressler makes art about the size of a postcard. Born in Herborn, Germany, Tina works as an artist and art instructor in the San Francisco Bay Area. She holds a degree in Science from Justus-Liebig-Universität Giessen, Germany and expands upon that background in her art. Her paintings explore a rhythmic dimension by integrating sacred geometry with organic, structured accidents.

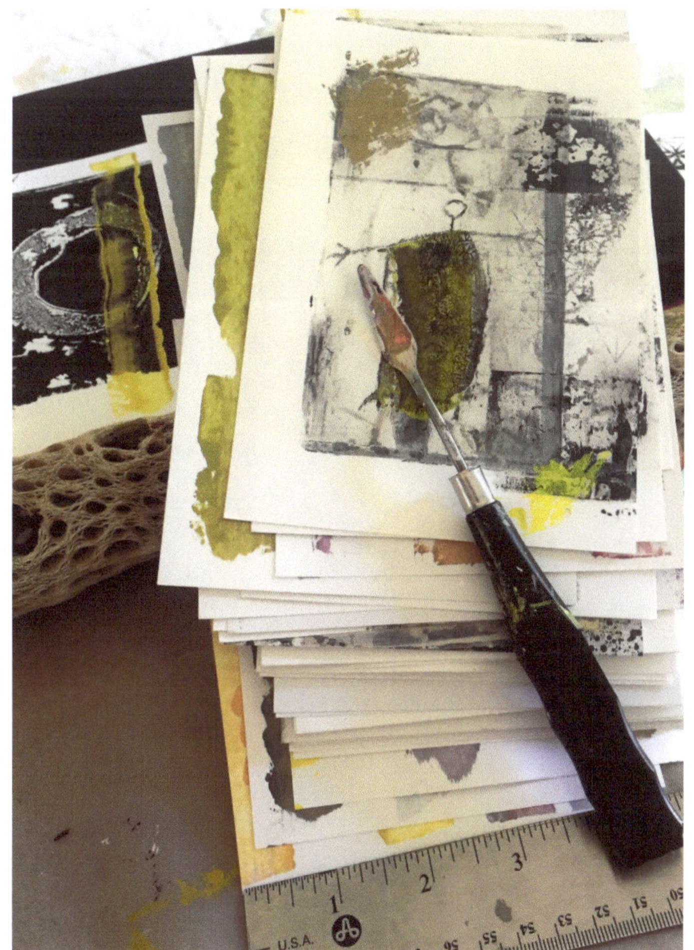

Tina Pressler, "Pranayama Beams"

Pressler most recently exhibited at the San Luis Obispo Museum of Art, the Transmission Gallery in Oakland and the ArtHouse in Sacramento. Selected prints are available through Williams Sonoma and Pottery Barn.

"The power of small format paintings. What started out as an experiment, quickly turned into a whole new level of exploration. My intention was simple. What if I shrink my tools, limit my palette, increase the speed I usually paint at, and focus only on the process of rhythm and repetition? A bit scary at first but super liberating. The unfamiliar setup turned into a trampoline of joy, fun and endless possibility. An innate workflow seemed to emerge as I let go of expectation, precision, certainty. The new process of applying paint to ten or more tiny pieces of paper, invited an opportunity to be surprised. And surprise is the foundation of creative flow. It creates a ripple effect. It turns chance into choice.

A couple of hundred pieces of structured accidents later, a river of potential remains to be refined and integrated."

- Tina Pressler

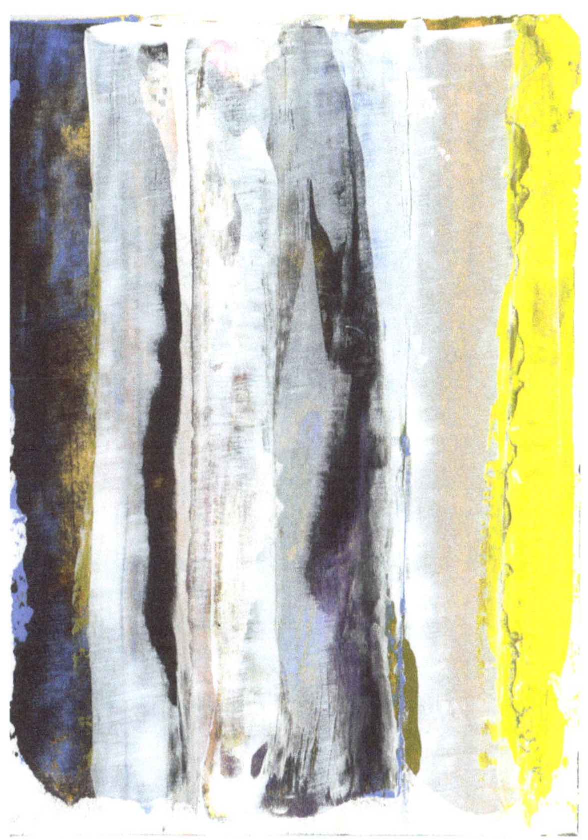

Tina Pressler, "Pranayama Beams # 8",
acrylic on paper, 4-1/2" x 6-1/2"

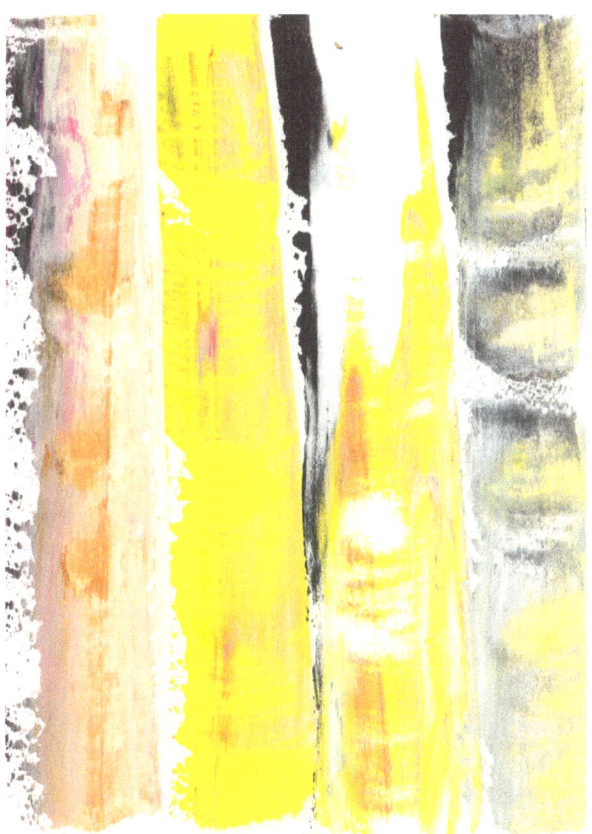

Tina Pressler, "Pranayama Beams # 9",
acrylic on paper, 4-1/2" x 6-1/2"

MYTH #4 - I SHOULD PAINT/DRAW/SCULPT EVERY DAY ON A SET SCHEDULE.

We often hear from creativity gurus that the only way to become artists is to be methodical; paint like clockwork every day. That's a load of bull. There's a lot to be said for sporadic art making. Professional artists don't simply paint all day, or even every day. They've developed the rhythm that works for them, and you'll find your own rhythm if you allow it to happen.

"The only reason for time is so that everything doesn't happen at once."
Albert Einstein

If you are just getting started or trying to get back into the studio after a dry spell, I suggest you do whatever you can to integrate your work into your daily life. You may need to do that while you're raising children or have a full time job. That may mean making art on your lunch hour if you're at work, or on the kitchen counter, while dinner is cooking. That's perfect and you should do it.

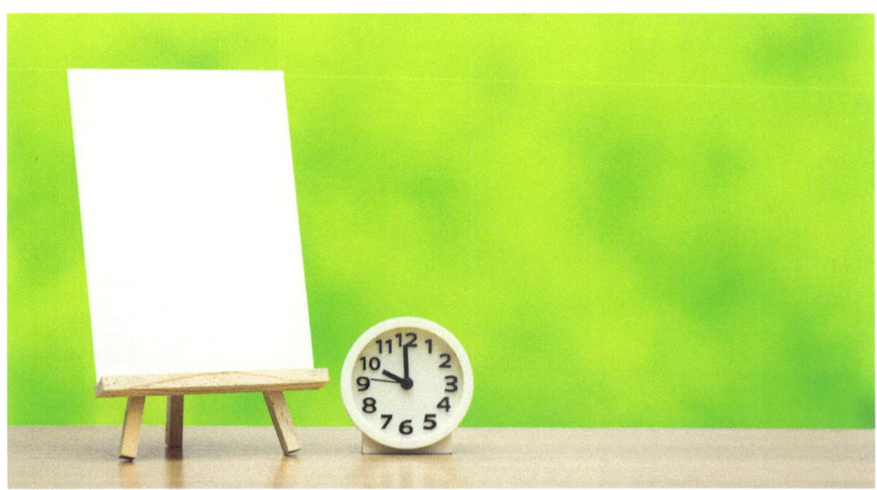

When I was a young painter, I had other "day" jobs. I felt like I never had enough time to make art. So I decided I would keep a log of all my time doing art-related stuff. I gave myself credit for reading art books and magazines, going to galleries and museums, shopping for art supplies during my lunch break and of course, making art. As it turns out, I was spending two-thirds of my time on art-related things and about one-third of my time on day jobs to support myself. That could be the reason I didn't have a winter coat for two years. Thirty years later and now I have administrative duties to run the studio and my art and teaching practice. The actual time of hands-on painting is about the same. Funny, huh?

Periodically I sequester myself somewhere, either in my studio with a big "do not disturb" sign or at an artist's retreat, and I produce a large volume of work. In a kind of work frenzy, I produce 12 to 14 hours a day and do nothing but paint, paint, paint for about two to three weeks. I call these my private painting retreats. I even put them on my calendar. I literally get up in the morning, pull on my painting clothes that are right on the floor by the bed, make the coffee and take it into the studio and start painting. I paint until I can't stand up anymore and then I go to bed. The next day I repeat the process. Periodically I take a shower and brush my teeth. I don't visit friends, have lunch with my pals, work on the computer or watch TV. I eat meals in the studio while looking at the work. I do nothing else.

My private retreats create a kind of flow for me. I produce a lot of work, some of it finished, some of it just started and it sustains me

for a year or so. I can then go back to the work that I didn't finish
during the retreat. It's like the unfinished pieces are battery packs
that re-ignite the flow and that becomes the work I do on a more
day-to-day basis. The flow also gets into new stuff in the studio. It
kind of seeps into blank canvases and an entire series will come out
of it.

I have to have the intense retreat first though, to jumpstart the
process. This is my rhythm. I fought it for years. I tried to be a 9
to 5 artist. I tried to go to the studio at the same time every day and
work. As it turns out, that's not who I am as an artist.

Your rhythm may be daily, or weekly or every other Thursday. It's
important to discover your rhythm and work with it, not against it.
Once you accept your own natural creative rhythm, you can stop
feeling guilty about not conforming to someone else's idea of what
it means to be an artist.

"Jazz is rhythm and meaning."
Henri Matisse

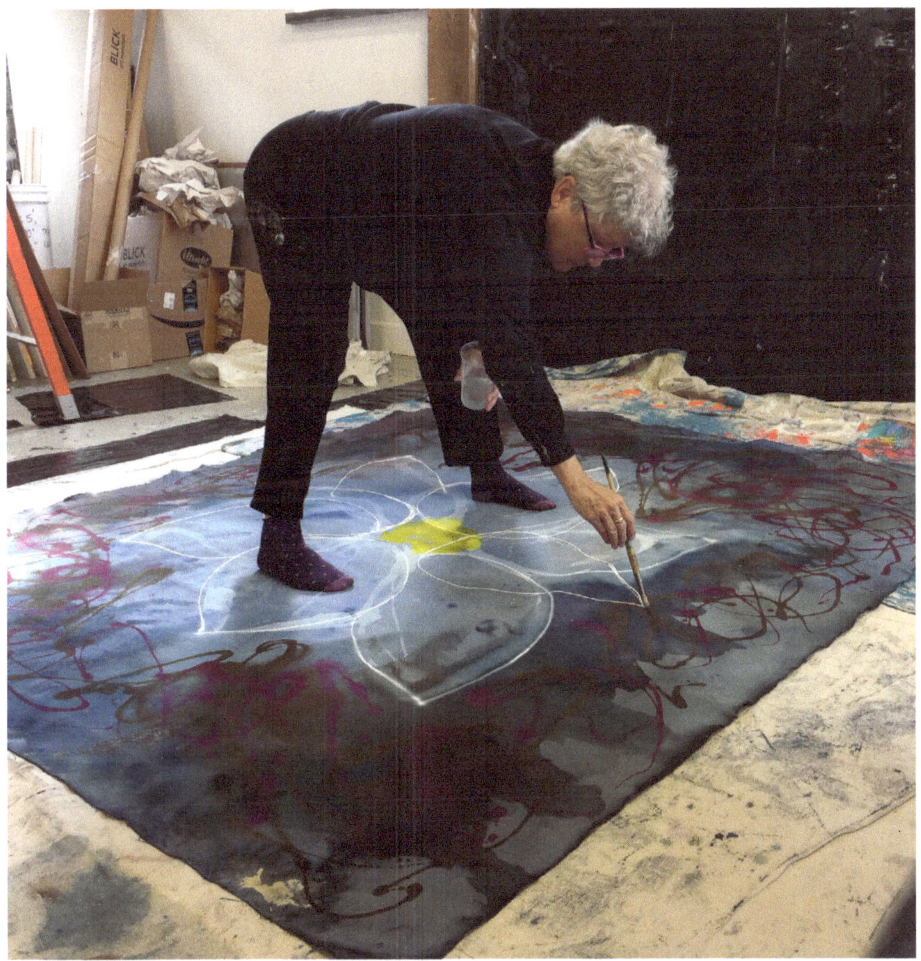

Working on the Lotus Series at the Golden Artist Colors™
Foundation, November 2017.

Oh the movies. Such an accurate interpretation of real life, right? Wrong, wrong, wrong. Being an artist in real life is nothing like the movies. A real artistic practice involves a lot more than painting in a messy studio and going to museum openings. A real artistic practice involves working on something on the corner of the table while the potatoes are cooking. Or maybe picking up art supplies on the way to the gym. Stopping the car on the way home from the grocery store to get a picture of that weird rock formation and then using that in a painting. And then there's all the time spent framing, filing, writing proposals, sweeping the studio, and on and on. They never show that in the movies. Why? Because it's boring. Who wants to watch an artist sweep the floor? Or stare at rock formations? An artistic practice is at least 50% non-painting time. And if you're an art teacher as I am, the non-painting time can be much higher.

Once you dispel these myths it's a lot easier to pick up the brush or pencil and just make something.

We're makers.

That's all we are.

Nothing special.

"Work like you don't need the money. Love like you've never been hurt. Dance like nobody's watching. "
Satchel Paige

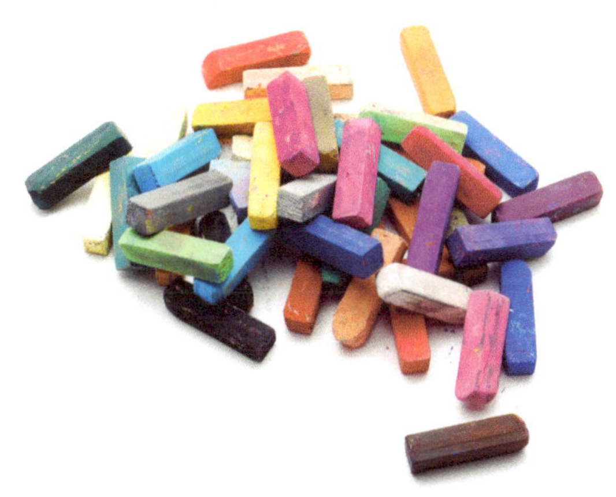

"You can't use up creativity. The more you use,
the more you have."

Maya Angelou

"MY MOTHER ALWAYS TOLD ME I WOULDN'T AMOUNT
TO ANYTHING BECAUSE I PROCRASTINATE.
I SAID, 'JUST WAIT.' "

JUDY TENUTA

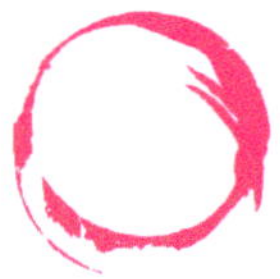

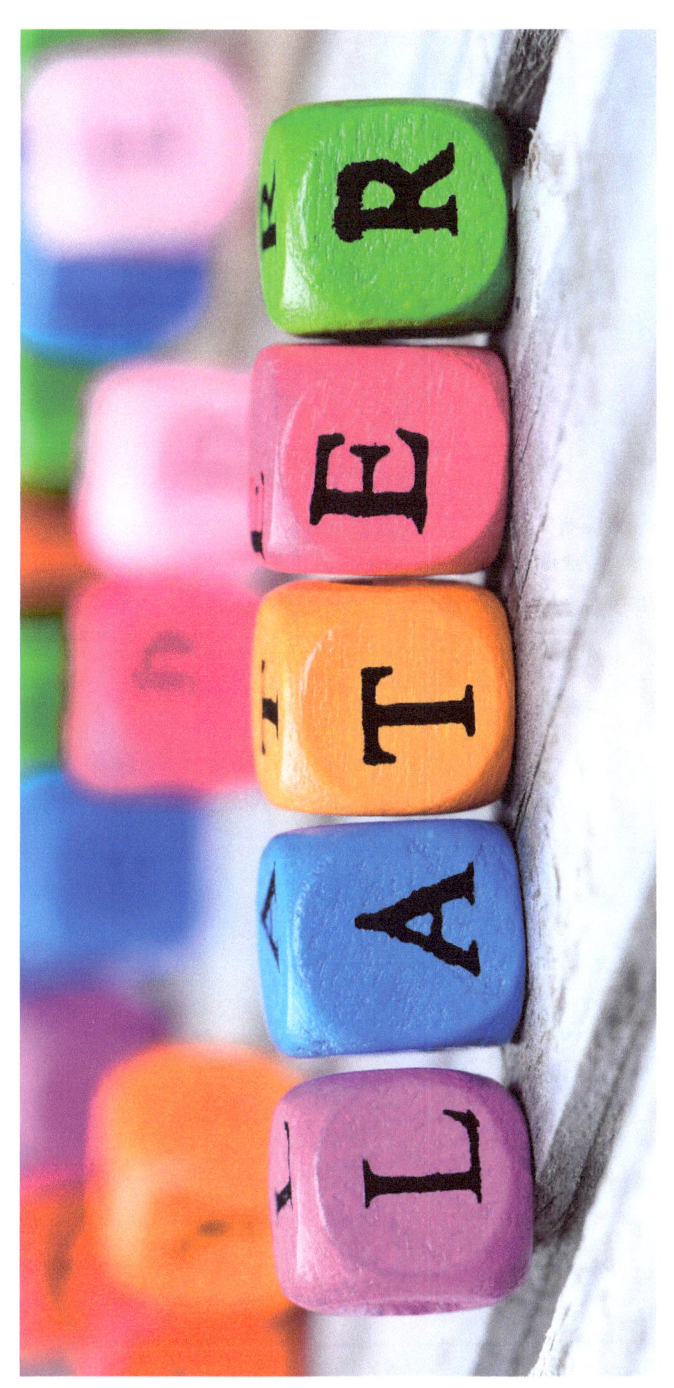

Chapter Three

But I Don't Wanna

Or

The Procrastination Station

So you know the first day of a diet, how hard it is not to eat that chocolate bar? Yeah it's hard, but then you force yourself to stay the course. You look at that little red dress in size 10 that you bought in anticipation of winning at this diet thing. It's just waiting for you and you force yourself to eat celery. Blech. But then a day or two goes by and you look that chocolate bar in the eye and you say, "you're not getting the better of me, you devil. I'll beat you. Yes I will." As Stanley Tucci said in *The Devil Wears Prada*, you gird your loins and prepare for battle.

When you just think about making stuff, instead of actually making it – that's what's happening, my friend. You are at battle with the Devil and the Devil's name is Procrastination.

I know this battle well because I've been fighting it for over 25 years. I'm a professional working artist and I battle Procrastination on a daily basis. I am constantly at war. I can hear you saying, oh my God, she's still battling this? Doesn't it get easier? Doesn't Procrastination eventually give up and just go away? Nope.

It. Never. Goes. Away.

Now before you throw your hands up in the air and admit defeat, let me tell you that this is a battle that I enjoy. No, I'm not masochistic and I don't enjoy existential angst but I do love to win. I love the feeling that I get right after I beat Procrastination. And I do beat it, over and over again. Damn I'm good. Yep, I'm bragging about it. But let me tell you, no one is going to brag for you and that's one of the ways you beat Procrastination. You brag on yourself. You pump yourself up. You fake it 'til you make it.

I don't care if you get one pencil line down on paper. You have beat Procrastination. For one ten-minute segment you won. YOU WON.

Do you have any idea how many people just give up on their dreams of making art? They get defeated by Procrastination one time and they give up. Not us, pal. You and me get ready for battle every day. We go to the mattresses.

"Resistance is always lying and always full of shit."
Steven Pressfield

Steven Pressfield, about whom I cannot say enough good things - he's a real mensch – wrote extensively about this in his book *The War of Art*. Read it. He compares Procrastination, or what he calls Resistance, to a natural force like gravity. And I think he's right. It's kind of like the yin and yang of creativity. You can't have all that juicy goodness without a little bad juju. You can't get to the chewy core of creativity without biting through the hard outer shell. The trick is to not let the hard outer shell defeat you.

Just bite harder, baby.

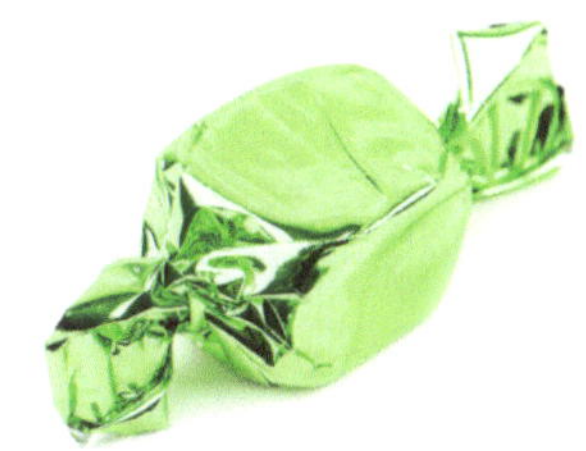

Okay so this is all well and good but how do we put this into practical terms? What can you do to defeat Procrastination? Here are a few tips:

Start looking at your art practice as a necessity instead of a luxury. You don't forget to brush your teeth do you? Well, your art practice is easily as important as your teeth.

Reward yourself. Hey, I'm all about the ends justifying the means. If it means that you get stuff done then by golly bribe yourself! You want to go to Hawaii for Christmas? Not until you get those four watercolors done, sister! You see where I'm going with this?

Set a timer. In my online class The 20 Minute Artist™ the projects are set up to be done in segments of twenty minutes or less. When you set the timer for yourself you MUST stop at the end of twenty minutes. Or start with ten. But you must stop when the timer dings. It's kind of like taking a test in school. The timer goes off and all pencils go down. This particular idea works amazingly well.

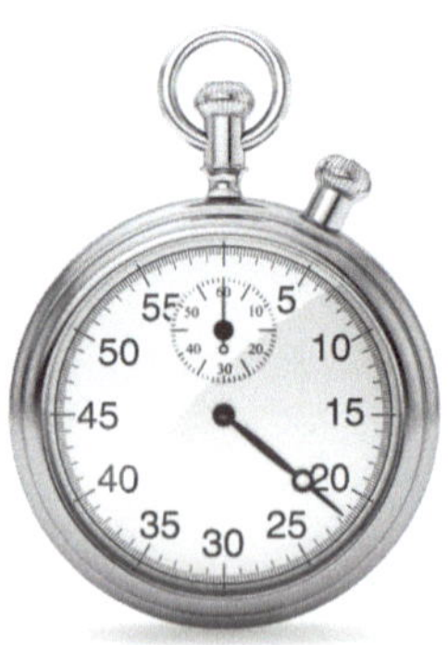

Why? Because you are tricking Procrastination. Procrastination doesn't know you're only planning on working for a few minutes. Wait, what? "You're going to stop after ten minutes and not feel guilty about it? No, no, NO!" screams Procrastination. "Everyone knows you must work long hours and suffer to get anywhere."

"Ten minutes is bullshit!" yells Procrastination. "You can't get anything done in ten minutes! You're a failure because you can't do the work - the long, hard, suffering work."

"Gee I'm sorry you feel that way", you say politely. "But I'm going for a walk. See ya!"

Just put your brush or pencil or scissors down at the end of those ten or twenty minutes and give Procrastination the middle finger. Take that you old devil.

Keep at it in ten or twenty-minute segments a day, every other day; just be cool about it. Pretty soon Procrastination gives up and slinks off the minute you pick up a brush. Because it knows you've beat it. It knows you've won the battle. It has to go find another artist to hassle.

Before you know it, you're working an hour, or two hours or five hours at a whack.

Just like the rockstar that you are.

And speaking of ten-minute segments. Please, please give up the idea that you have to be in a "studio" with "art materials" to create "art". That's a lot of air quotes people. But this is an important point. Art and creativity do not rely on a special place or special materials. I'm sure I've said this before but it bears repeating.

There is a long and illustrious list of artists – some famous, some not so – who created with whatever they had at hand. Picasso and oilcloth, Robert Rauschenberg and old tires, Howard Finster and toilet seats, Betty Saar and discarded jewelry, Joseph Cornell and thrift store castoffs. The list goes on and on.

The place you create doesn't matter either.   Henri Matisse created his entire Jazz series from his bed or wheelchair. And of course you've heard of the little yellow house where Vincent van Gogh lived. You've seen the painting of his bedroom. Well he was in the bedroom when he painted it, right? If the bedroom was good enough for Vincent, then it ought to be good enough for you.

Get a buddy. Get yourself a pal and make a deal with him or her. I'll show you mine if you show me yours kinda thing. You don't necessarily have to work together in the same space. Heck, with all the modern technology we have at our disposal, you don't even have to be in the same hemisphere! But having someone to be accountable to is amazing. It's almost as if you hate to let them down more than yourself, so you get the work done so you'll have something to show. Something to discuss. Something to be proud of.

Okay, so now you are armed against Procrastination.

You've got street smarts and you can duke it out with the big P.

One word of caution, don't get cocky. Don't ever let your guard down.

You have to stay vigilant because if you don't, Procrastination will come back with a vengeance.

Keep fighting my friend.

"The two most powerful warriors are patience and time."
Leo Tolstoy

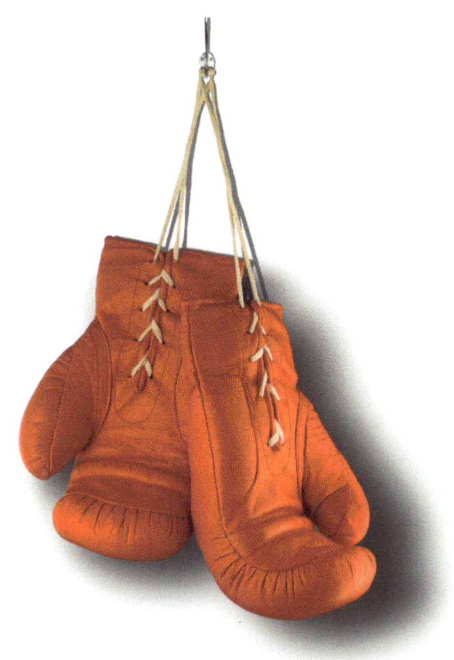

"ORIGINALITY IS NOTHING BUT JUDICIOUS IMITATION."

VOLTAIRE

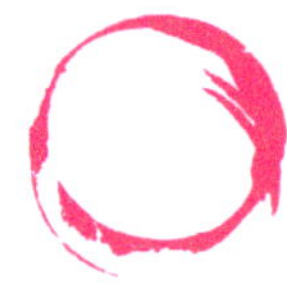

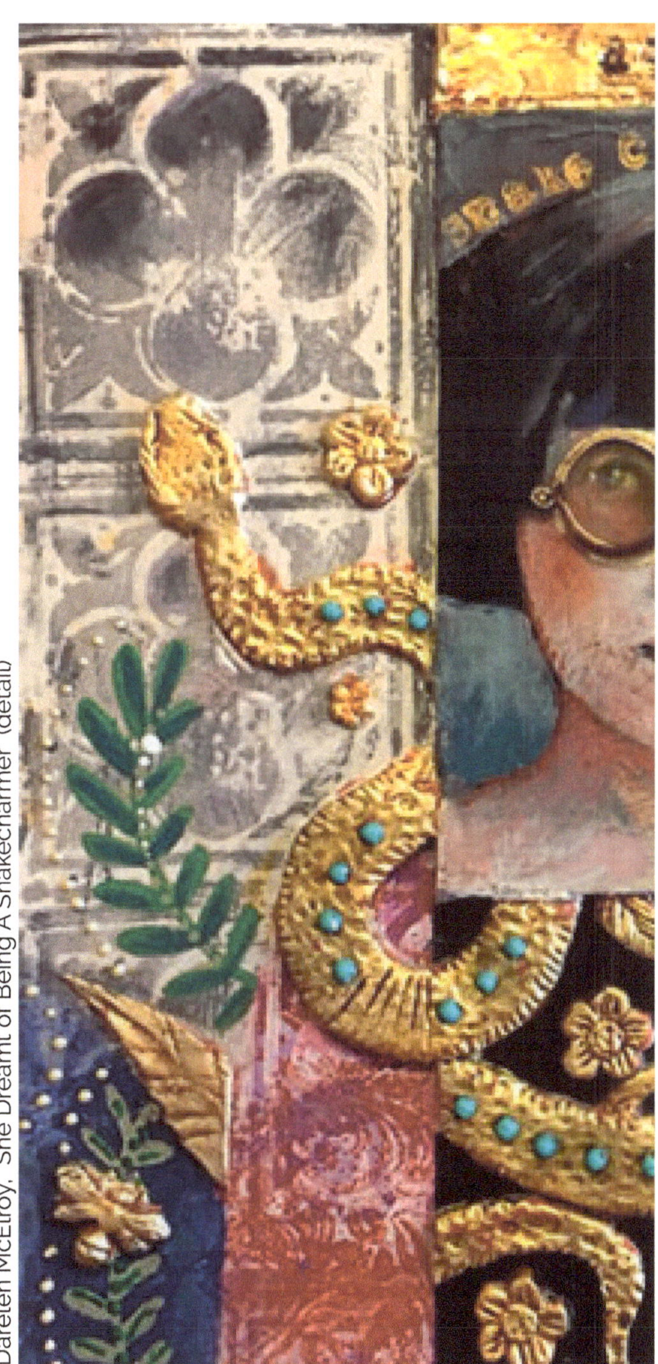

Chapter Four

Goats
and
Sacred Gold

ARE you worried about your skills? Think you need to spend 10,000 hours to get really good at painting or drawing and THEN you'll be an artist? Let's shoot down one Myth of the Artist here. The one that says everyone who wants be an artist has to paint like Leonardo Da Vinci or draw like Michelangelo.

That model works great if you're trying to create High Renaissance or representational art. If all you're interested in is making art that looks like a thing then you need those skills.

You can find a teacher and study for a couple of years. If you work hard enough, you may indeed learn to draw and paint things that look like they are supposed to. But there's no guarantee that it will satisfy that longing to feel the tingle in the pit of your stomach.

That tingle in your stomach or the hair standing up on the back of your neck, that comes from an encounter with the Other. The numinous. Pure creativity. You've probably felt it, standing in front of a painting you love. You can't quite explain it but you know it when you feel it.

I feel like that in front of Mark Rothko's paintings. Something deep inside me wakes up and my whole body feels tingly, alive. I often feel tears well up when I look at his work. Why? It's just paint on canvas. But for me, there's an indescribable feeling emanating from those canvases. There is no skillful drawing, no fancy paint handling. There are just luminous fields of color, hovering on the canvas.

Not everyone reacts to Rothko like this. I have stood in the museum in front of his painting and seen people just whiz by, glancing at the canvas and then dashing on to the next painting around the corner. Stop! I want to yell at them. Stop and see this magic right in front of your eyes!

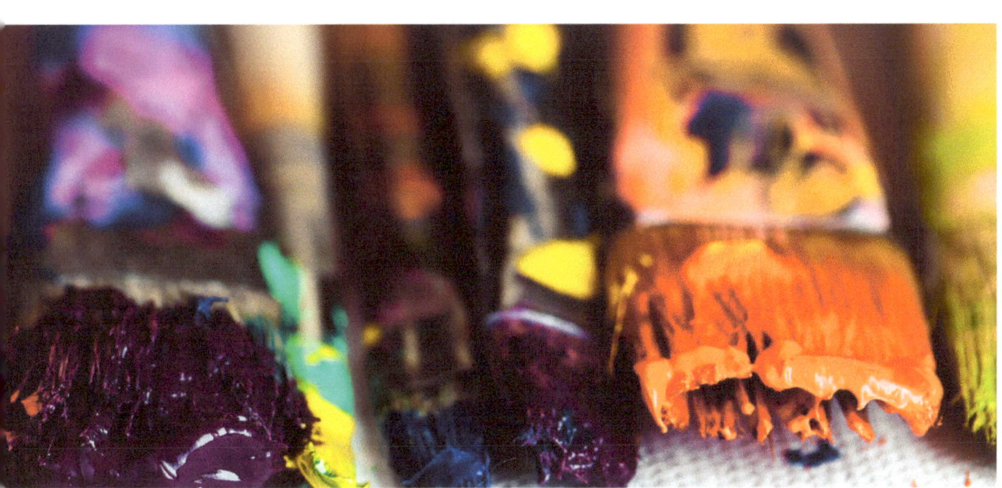

Why am I brought to the edge of rapture by his paintings and the next person doesn't even bother to stop? Ah, that's the beauty of art. It's subjective. It depends entirely on your personal engagement with it. Art is all about personal connection, a one-to-one with the art.

You see, we are no longer living in the Middle Ages or even the High Renaissance. Obviously, right? Why then do we still have these outdated attitudes about what is "good" art? At a time when the vast majority of the populace was illiterate, art served a practical purpose - to illustrate a story. Most art created before the modern era – roughly before 1850 – was meant to tell a story or copy reality.

But modern art, anything made after 1850 or so, has to be seen in a new context. It's a form of personal expression. It is no longer only meant to serve a practical purpose. Modern art can be made of anything. It can be made in any way. Modern art doesn't have to be a perfect replication of a thing - it can be about a personal connection between the artist and the artwork.

In modern art, expression in its purest form comes from a place of authenticity without an attachment to craft. The great artist and writer, Wassily Kandinsky, in his book *Concerning the Spiritual in Art* puts forth the idea that artists should not be tied to the real world. That they should not concern themselves with copying reality. That they should be allowed to express themselves from their own inner world, much like musicians do. He also thought that abstraction was the highest form of art and I agree with him.

Look, anyone can learn to draw and paint things that look like things, if they are given good solid instruction and take the time to practice. And everyone can create art that moves us, that is inspired. But sometimes the idea of getting it right, making it look like a thing, gets in the way of the truth. The artist works so hard at making it right that she loses the magic along the way.

Say you are madly in love with someone. You want to paint a portrait of that person but you lack the training to create a classical portrait. Take a photograph of your beloved on your smartphone. Put some music on that reminds you of the beloved. Now blow up the photograph so that you only see one eye or one ear or a piece of the chin. Just look at those shapes, get those shapes down on paper or canvas. Don't try to copy them, try to

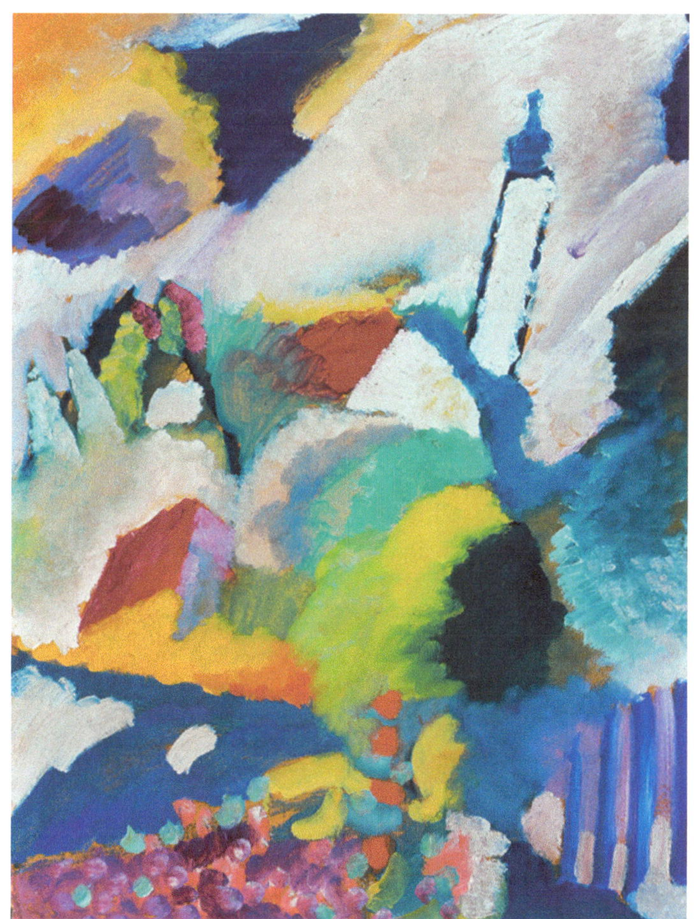

Wassily Kandinsky, "Murnau with Church", oil on canvas 1910

feel those shapes. Close your eyes and imagine he or she is kissing you. What color does that feel like? Put it on the paper. Does it need short, dashed brushstrokes? Or long wispy brushstrokes? Where were you when you first met? On the beach? A crowded city street? In a bar? Close your eyes and re-imagine the scene. What does it feel like? Thick paint? Collaged bits of glass?

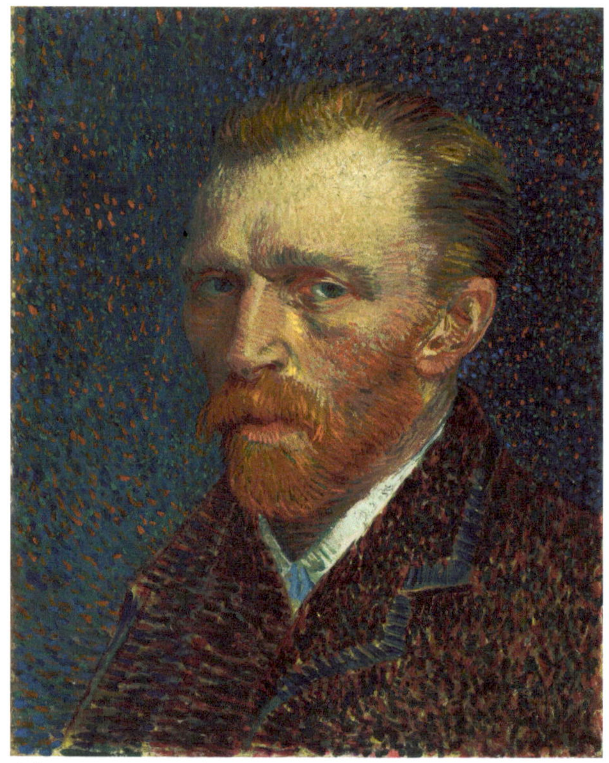

Vincent van Gogh, 'Self Portrait', oil on canvas, 1887

These are just ways to begin. What I'm trying to get across to you is that you need to find the authentic feeling and express it. The authenticity will far outweigh any lack of technique.

Think of Vincent Van Gogh's paintings. He was untrained but passionate. His passion became his training. His paintings are some of the most loved in the world. All painted by an artist who was never professionally trained.

Trust your feelings. The painting or drawing will fall into place if you are open to the feeling. You'll know it when you see it. You'll feel it. Me and Rothko - yes that feeling.

Joseph Beuys was a German artist living and working in the mid 20th century. He is considered to be one of the most important artists of that era. His work primarily involved performance pieces like *How To Explain Pictures To A Dead Hare* and *I Like America and America Likes Me.* I won't go into a long explanation here about Beuys or these works. Except to say that they involved fat, felt and sometimes gold leaf and honey. You can look him up online and get quite a bit of information. What I will stress is that this very important artist did not use representational means or high skill to express himself. His work was deeply significant, not only to himself, but to modern art in general. And he didn't need exceptional drawing skills or 10,000 hours of painting practice. Look up his work. Maybe it speaks to you, maybe not. It is important enough to be collected by museums all over the world. In my opinion, the impact of his work on modern art can't be denied. And yet, there are those who say it was all just a bunch of hogwash.

Again, there's that personal connection to art rearing its head. One person's treasure is another person's trash. That's the beauty of art in the modern world. It's personal.

It can be anything. Made out of anything. By anyone, anywhere, at any age.

Emily Kame Kngwarreye was an indigenous Australian artist who didn't start painting until she was 80 years old. She had a great deal of success in her short career. I found her work when visiting Miami Art Basel. The intricacy of the work just knocked me out. Once I started looking into her history, I realized that she had not even picked up a brush until she was 80 years old. I love that! And the pictures of her painting – outside, seated on the ground with a goat next to her – really spoke to me. Why? Because one of the biggest obstacles I hear from my students is that they have nowhere to paint. Really? How about sitting on the ground with a goat? Emily's work has sold at Sotheby's for hundreds of thousands of dollars. She didn't have a studio. She didn't have any training. She just had a passion to create.

If you feel strongly about something it doesn't matter how you express it. The most important piece of this is that you tell the truth. You find a way to express the feeling with authenticity.

Which brings up a question. What do you love? What material speaks to you?

If you disregard notions of what "art" really is - what substance would you work with?

Here are some things you could try:

Whatever is in the kitchen cupboard. Beans, macaroni, aluminum foil. I've made art with all of them. And so have a lot of other artists.

Sand, rocks, tree bark, sticks, grass, twigs. Native populations have been using these materials for thousands of years. In fact, Navajo sand paintings are considered part of a ceremonial healing practice and are meant to be obliterated after the ceremony, the sand returned to the earth.

Newspaper, old magazines, fabric scraps. The art of collage has a long and illustrious history. Hannah Hoch, Kurt Schwitters, Henri Matisse, Max Earnst, Picasso - the list of famous artists who used collage in their work is far too long to mention here.

And all you need is some glue and a pair of scissors.

Junk. Plain old junk you find in the trash. Smashed aluminum cans, old buttons, broken jewelry, odd bits of machinery, car parts, cast off pieces of wood. Louise Nevelson made sublime, exotic sculptures with wooden boxes and bric-a-brac she found. The wonderful artist Joseph Cornell created an entire body of work using junk and debris he found on the street and thrift store finds.

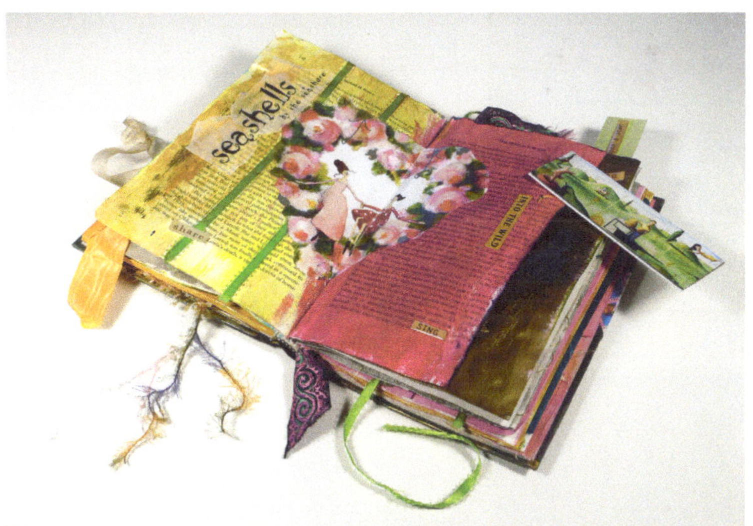

Tesia Blackburn, "Artist's Book", acrylic paint, book and found objects

His boxes are like small universes - each with a particular story.

You don't need any special materials or tools to create art.

You just need the willingness to express yourself without worrying about the outcome.

Darlene McElroy, born and raised in Southern California, is descended from an old New Mexico family of artists and storytellers. She has been deeply influenced by the summers she spent growing up on her family's ranch in Santa Fe where the rich tapestry of Hispanic life filled the nights and brightly colored the days. Her paternal grandfather was an artist on Catalina Island who exposed her to art as a life style, introduced her to color and the narrative in art. She currently lives in Santa Fe where she enjoys the skies, the color and the art.

"Let the beauty of what you love be what you do."
Rumi

"I approach art as a treasure hunter, mad scientist and storyteller. Because I tend to paint in thin layers I use found and cast objects along with deconstructed stencils and crazy paint skins to build up my paintings. Every piece I create is an adventure in learning new tricks and adding to my art arsenal. If I don't have molding material I will use the wax cover on cheese or clay, if I don't have resist material, then I will use butter, and so on. Wasted paint, never! It will go in a mold or on a texture plate to become a cast object or a paint skin. This is the magic of art that appeals to me."

- Darlene McElroy

She Dreamt of Being a Snake Charmer, 12" x 12" mixed media on panel. Originally when I finished this, the girl had painted glasses. However, a friend gave me a box of her mother's things and the little wire glasses were in it.

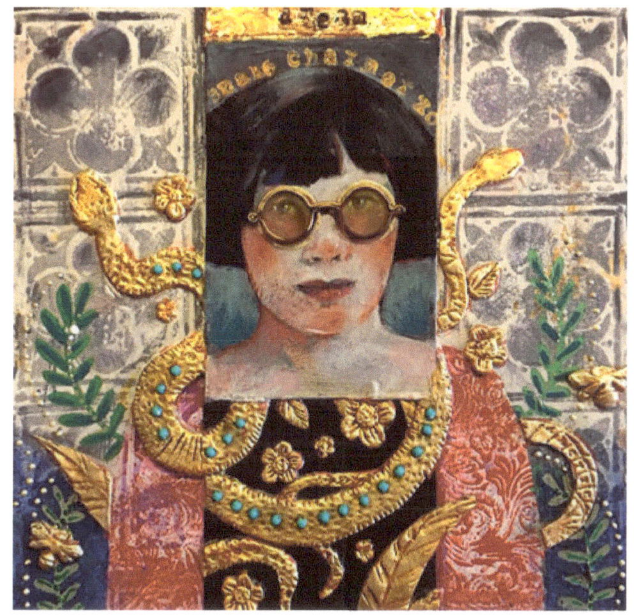

My Nights are More Beautiful than Your Days, 24" x 24" mixed media on panel. I scored a dozen old tomb rubbings on Etsy. I added objects from a box of jewels, chains, etc. that was left on my doorstep like a giant Christmas present. I put my knight in an ornate garden design with bugs cast with paint and a smile on his face.

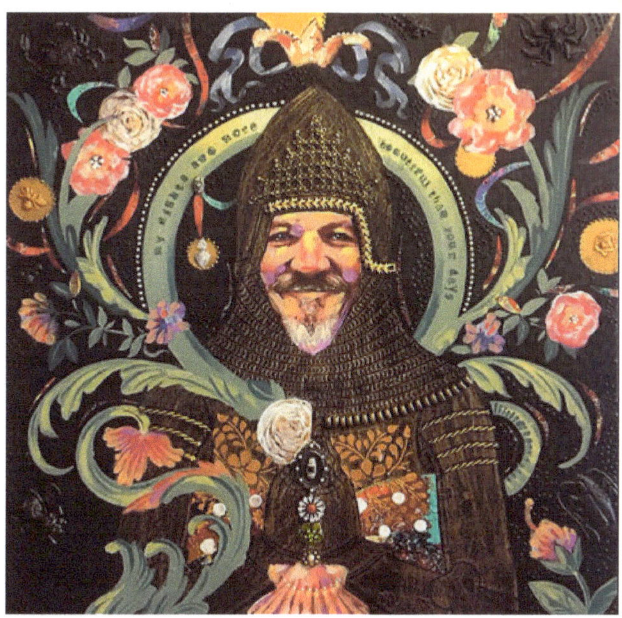

"Follow your bliss."

Joseph Campbell

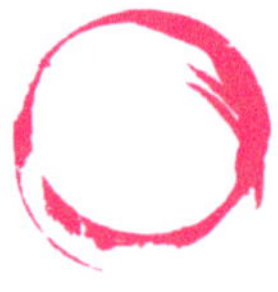

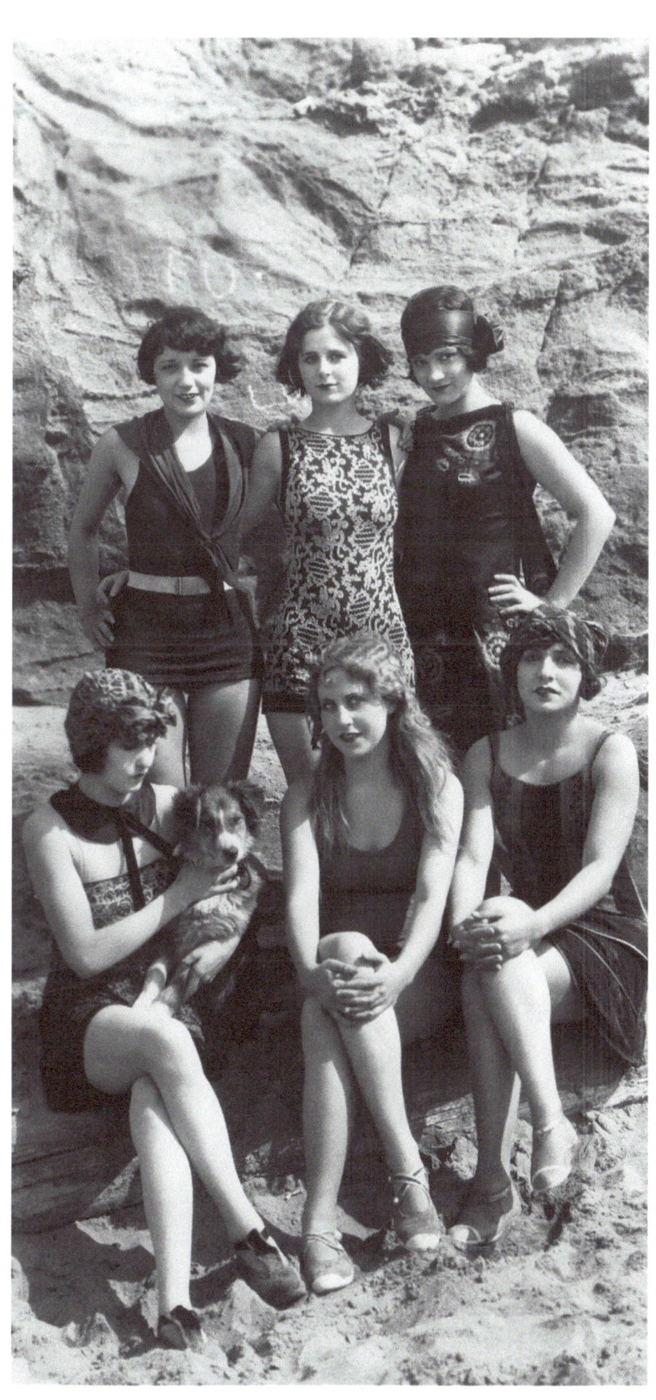

Chapter Five

Hang With Your Gang

IMAGINE this (or maybe it's even happened to you). You're at a dinner party with your pals from work. Let's say you're an investment banker, or a kindergarten teacher or a basketball coach. Your pals from work don't know much about your side hustle as an artist. They may know you "dabble" in the arts but that's about it.

You can converse with them at length about banking, educational curricula, or shooting free throws. But are they the ideal group to talk to about why you love Cerulean Blue more than Cobalt Blue? Or why, in your opinion, Vincent van Gogh was the world's best painter? Or whether you should use acrylics or oils?

Probably not.

Granted everyone will have something to say about your art. It just won't be that helpful if it's not coming from folks who understand what you're trying to do.

You need to find your tribe - your posse - folks who talk your talk and walk your walk.

You wouldn't ask an investment banker to teach kindergarten would you? Unless she has a degree in childhood education she's just not suited for that job.

And yet every day I hear students say that their husband/brother/

sister/wife/aunt/hairdresser didn't like or understand their painting. So maybe that means the painting is bad. Maybe you shouldn't be creating art anyway because you have no talent. After all, your brother, the investment banker, doesn't understand what you're trying to do.

Now before you get your hackles up and take me to task for being an elitist let me explain. I am not saying that your family and friends are ignorant or uninformed. They may have the best intentions. What I am saying is that unless they engage in a creative pursuit on a regular basis they don't speak the same language we do. Even though everyone has the ability to be creative, if they don't acknowledge those abilities or talk about them, they probably won't get what you're doing.

And you're doing them a disservice by asking them for their opinion.

Why?

Have you ever noticed how some people just clam up in front of art? Especially abstract art. I've been an abstract painter for a long time and believe me, I've seen it over and over again. Generally speaking, most people feel uncomfortable expressing their feelings about art. It's not that they're stupid or uninformed. It's just not a familiar language. Unless they create something themselves, they're just not sure what to say.

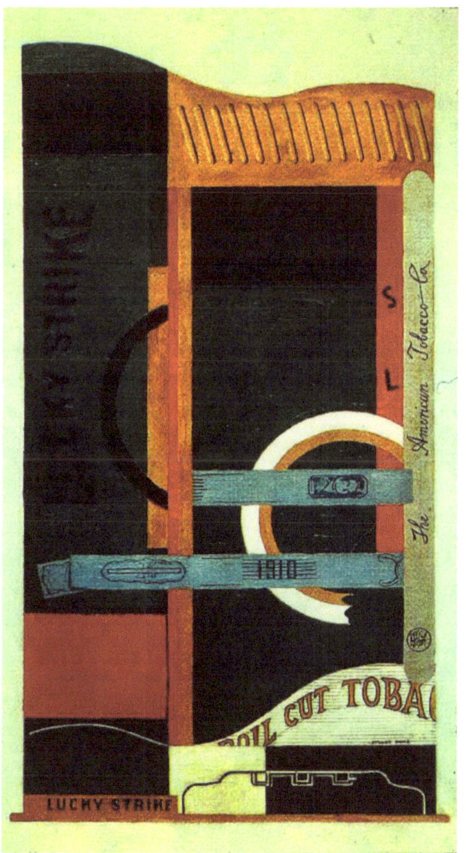

Stuart Davis "Lucky Strike"
oil on canvas, 1921.

"It looks like a dinosaur."

"Gee, that's a nice purple square thingie right there."

Or my all-time favorite, "How long did it take you to paint this?"

By asking your family or friends, those who don't create art on a regular basis, to critique your work, you are making them uncomfortable. Even though neither you nor they realize it. And the end result can be unsettling or even disastrous. If someone close to you has a negative reaction to something you created, even though they may not be qualified to critique it, it can dampen your creative spirit, or worse yet, kill it. And the next time you feel that creative urge coming on you may ignore it.

So what to do?

Find your tribe. Hang with your gang. Chill with your peeps.

Join the museum and go to the openings. Take a drawing class at the local college. Engage in some online groups around art. Get out and mingle with like-minded people.

And then ask for some feedback.

I know from experience how tough it can be to find people who don't roll their eyes when I blather on about how Quinacridone Magenta has that lovely bluish undertone. Or how the ink was applied on some of Edgar Degas' monotypes. And did you see the Matisse exhibit? Wasn't it to die for?

Remember, you're speaking a new language. The language of color, shapes, textures, lines. Hang out with other people who like to make stuff and who speak your language. If you're in love with creating, find folks who speak that language of love.

Believe me, it's blissful.

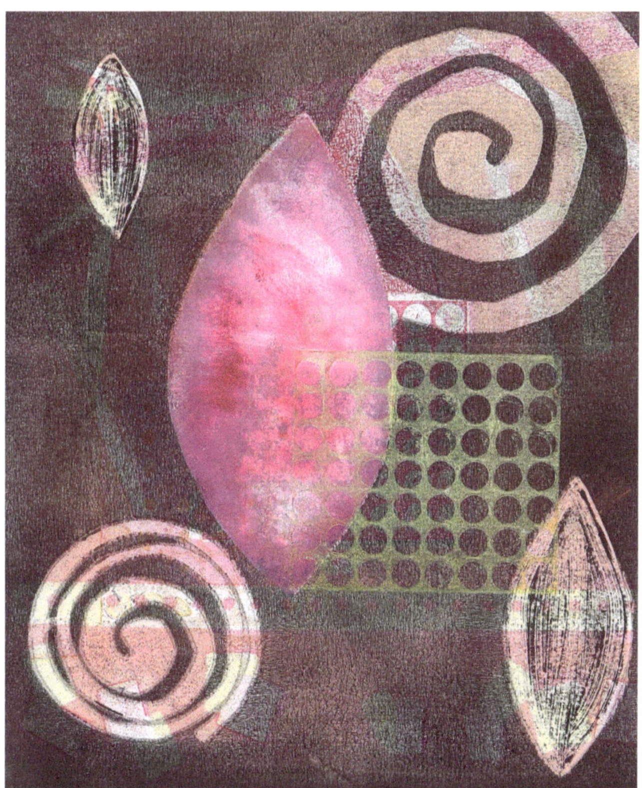

Tesia Blackburn, "Live, Laugh, Love #5", monotype on paper, 22" x 30" 2016

""Don't look at your feet to see if you are
doing it right. Just dance."

Anne Lamott

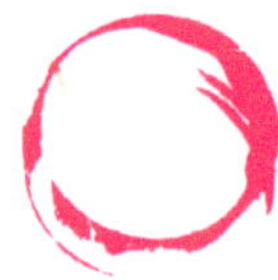

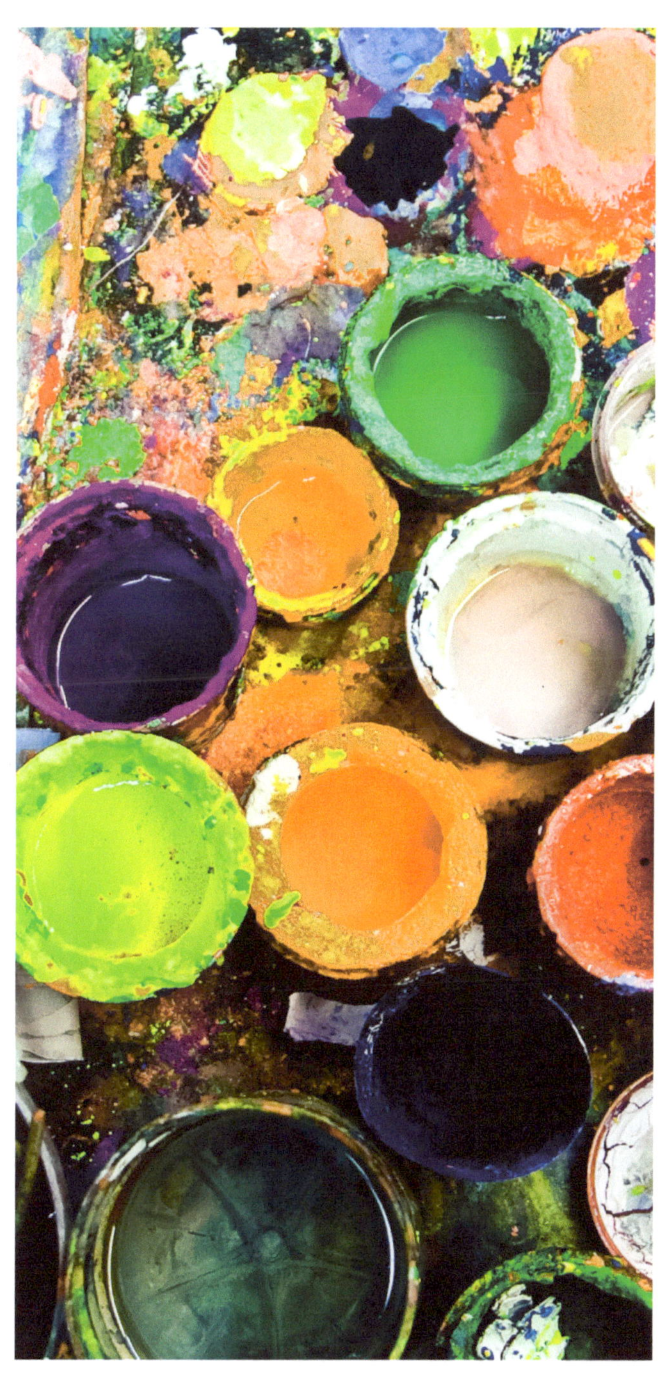

Chapter Six

The School of Life

Or

Why Shopping At Macy's Means You're Already An Artist

LIVING in San Francisco I see all kinds of people every day. Hipsters, working moms, bike messengers, business people in suits, café baristas, techno geeks and nerds and everything in between. Each and every one of these people put themselves together for the day. They got up in the morning and picked out a shirt, some socks, a skirt, a pair of leggings and maybe a baseball cap. They decided on that jacket with those earrings and that scarf.

What does all of this have to do with being an artist? Plenty. You see, everyone already has all the skills they need to make art. We make decisions about color, texture, shape, lines, and composition every day, all day long. We just happen to think it has nothing to do with creativity or making art.

Nothing could be further from the truth.

When I first tell this to beginning students in my classes they look at me with their mouths open. Stunned. It's as if I've introduced them to a foreign language. In a way I have. It's just that they've been speaking this language all along without realizing it. It's like the first time I went to Paris and was astonished that all the children spoke French so well. Well, duh! This is the exact same thing. You have been speaking art lingo all along and you just didn't know it.

Don't believe me? See if this rings true. I've sent you to Macy's or Saks or whatever department store you like with my favorite sweater and I've asked you to get me a scarf to go with it. Not to

match it. To go with it. Take your best friend with you on this
shopping trip. Does your conversation go something like this?

*"Oh this would look good with that sweater because it has pink in it.
See those little flecks of pink? It picks up the pink lines in the sweater.
Hmmm, but the pink might be too yellow. It's really more red. Let's
keep looking."*

That, my friend, is color theory in a
nutshell. You can see that the pink is
too yellow, or the blue is too green or
whatever. Trust your eyes. Your eyes
know color a lot better than you might
believe.

Now go back to the store and get me a
blouse to go with my purple nubby wool suit. Thanks by the way!
What kind of blouse are you looking for? Turtle neck sweater?
Nope. Why not? Because it's the wrong texture to go with a nubby
wool suit. I can hear you saying, "she'll need a silky blouse under
that suit. That will be perfect. Maybe a darker shade of purple, or a
purple that has some gray in it."

Geez, you're now talking color AND texture.

Do you see where I'm going with this? Neither of these examples is
beyond anyone reading this book. You just have to trust your gut.
Just take the instincts that you already have and put them on paper

or canvas. Color, texture, shape…it's all the same as shopping at Macy's.

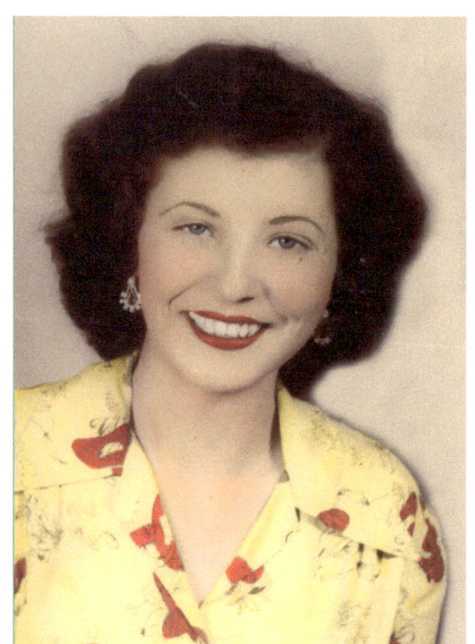
Dorothy Blackburn circa 1950.

My mom was a true Southern belle. She never left the house without lipstick. I was always amazed at how put together she was. She could take a giant fancy scarf, tie it into some kind of intricate knot and pin it to her shoulder with a big broach. She never considered herself artistic but she had the eye. She did the same thing with her home. The bedspread went with the towels in the bathroom and the accent pillow matched the rug.

I would bet that your home is put together just like my mom's. There is probably a comfy chair with a lamp and a table next to it. Your sofa probably faces the fireplace or the television with maybe a coffee table in front of it. You're composing your home. You're using compositional tools to make the space you live in work. So the traffic pattern works. So people can sit down and talk to each other easily. So you can see the television from the couch. You make these things work because you trust your instincts. You know that the area rug has to be just there under the couch. Why? Because you can sense when the composition is wrong.

Have you ever walked into someone's home and had an unquenchable desire to move a piece of furniture? You know the chair would look so much better if it was just angled a tiny bit. Or maybe they have too many tchotchkes? Or not enough tchotchkes? What's going on here?   It's your gut instinct telling you the composition is off or the color is wrong or one of a number of things.

We are all hard-wired with all the information we need to make art. We've been speaking this language all along and didn't know it.

See? I told you artists were not a special, elite group.

We're all artists.

All the time.

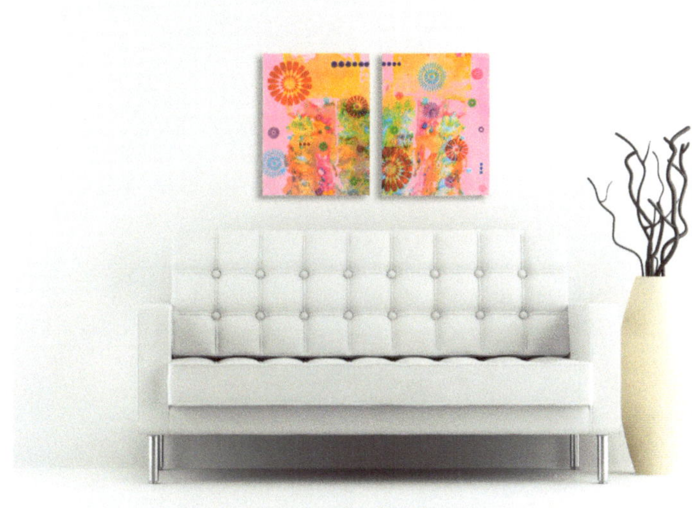

Tesia Blackburn, "Sunkissed I and II", acrylic on canvas

"Don't think about making art, just get it done. Let everyone else decide if it's good or bad, whether they love it or hate it. While they are deciding, make even more art."

Andy Warhol

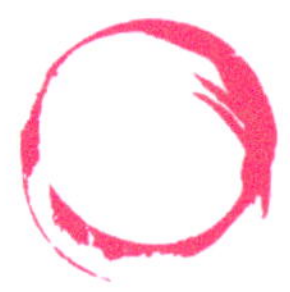

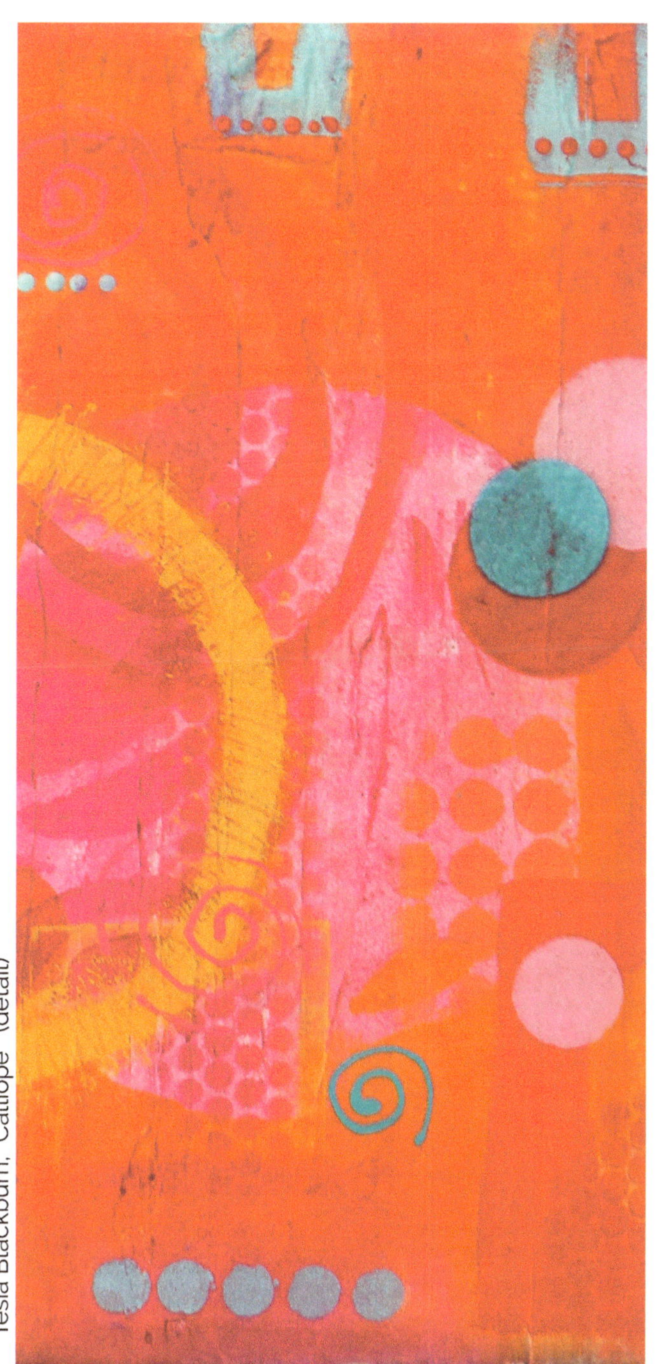
Tesia Blackburn, "Calliope" (detail)

Chapter Seven

You're Not Going to Solve Global Warming

So You Might As Well Make Art

LOOK, making art will not save the world. But it might save you.

I have this crazy idea that making art will make us happy, and being happy spreads positive energy. And spreading positive energy is a good thing.

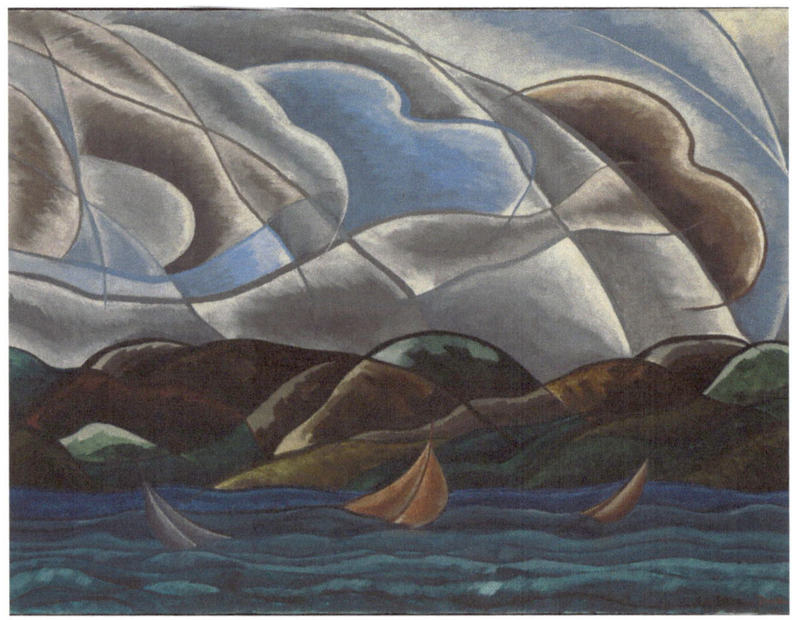

Arthur Dove, "Clouds and Water", oil on canvas, 1930

Actually it's not a crazy idea at all. I'm not alone in the notion that doing this stuff will make you feel better in the long run. From Psychology Today magazine to art therapy blogs, the word is out. Making art has a positive impact on our well being. It's no longer just anecdotes either. Studies have been done that show creating art impacts our physical and mental well being in a number of ways.

It reduces stress, elevates your mood and increases your ability to solve problems. Creating art can increase your self-esteem too.

But what about all those "tortured" artists, you may ask. I will go out on a limb and say that the percentage of tortured artists is about

the same of any other working population. In other words, there is
depression and mental illness in any field of endeavor. Artists just
get viewed through a different lens. And the "tortured" ones get all
the press.

There are hundreds of thousands of artists who are mentally
healthy and creating wonderful work. You don't have to buy into
the "tortured" myth of the artist.

In fact, I hope you don't.

"Art is an investigation."
Twyla Tharp

Instead, I want you to buy into the Myth of the Blissful Artist.
Creating art will create what I like to call a "bliss bubble". You
get a little jolt of pleasure every time you pick up a brush or a
pencil. It's almost like you're falling in love, over and over again.
Time seems to stand still and everything seems to glow.

Yes I know it's all very woo-woo. But trust me. Just try it.

Try making art without caring whether it solves any problems.

Try making art without caring if it's any good.

Try making art just for the hell of it.

Now let me be clear. You must set aside your ideas of making "good" art or "meaningful" art or any other adjective that you can come up with. You've got to set aside the idea that it has to be perfect.

Oh for God's sake, please don't try to make perfect art.

Instead, try to make something that's completely worthless. And maybe ugly. I know this sounds crazy but I promise, it will help. If you set out with the mindset that none of this matters, nothing you make really has an impact on the world, then you are free to do anything you want to do.

I know what you're thinking. "Why make it at all then? If it doesn't matter, why bother?"

Because you have to. Even if no one ever sees it. You must make it. Why? Because Inspiration needs to be expressed. Love and Joy need to be expressed.

And because it will make you happy. Isn't that enough of a reason?

Just make something with no expectations. Do it without any judgement. Don't worry if it's "good" or "meaningful" or any other yardstick of worth. It's worthy, believe me. If for no other reason than it delights you.

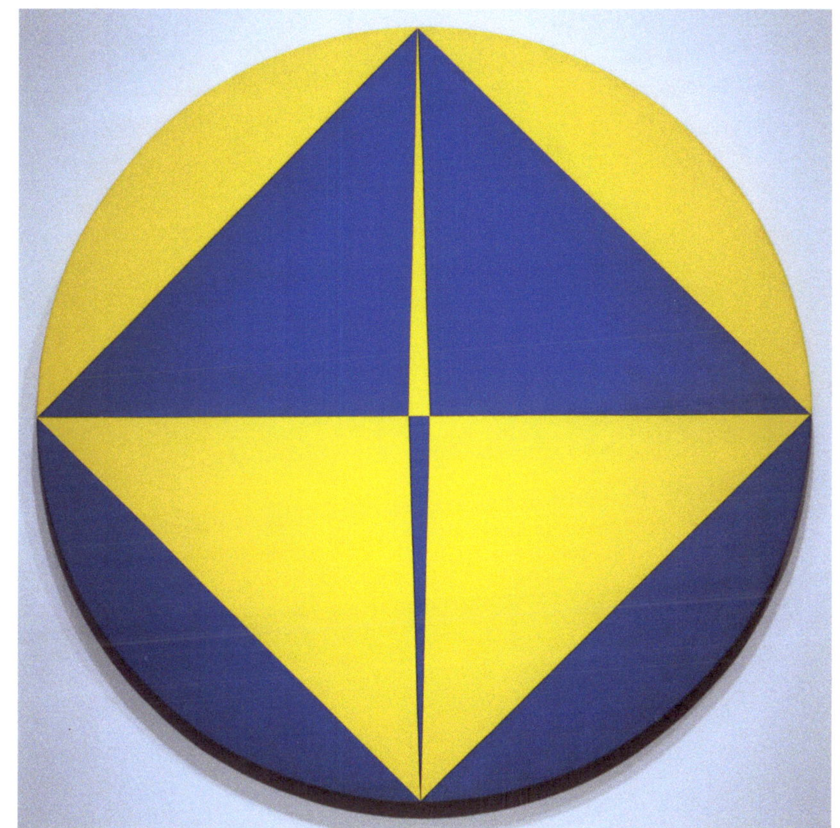

Carmen Herrera, "Rondo (Blue and Yellow" ,
acrylic on canvas, 1965

"Creativity is contagious. Pass it on."

Albert Einstein

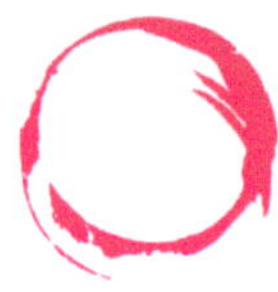

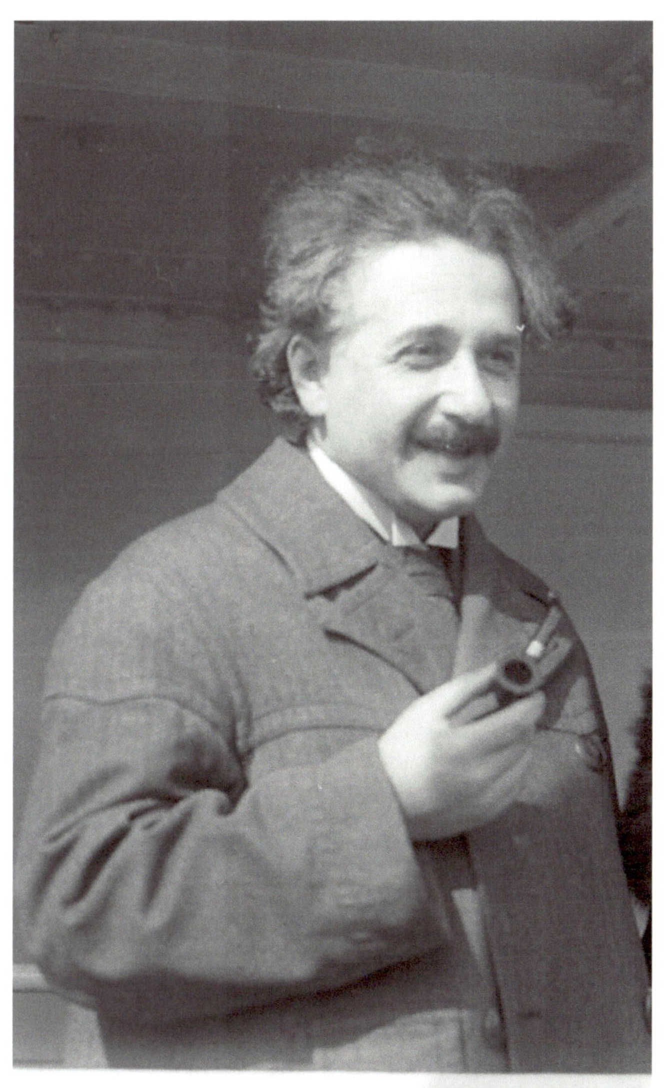

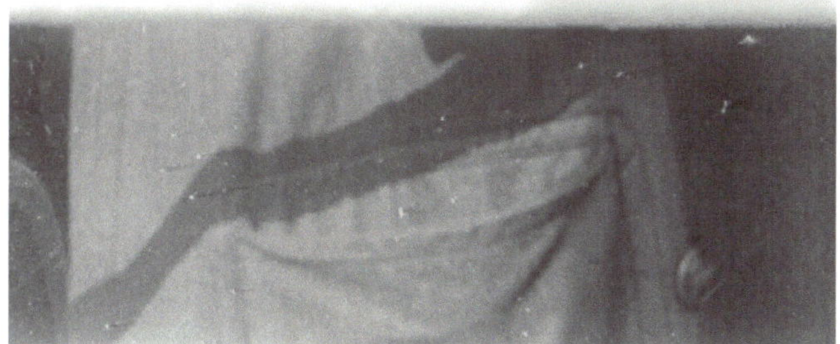

CHAPTER EIGHT

EINSTEIN AND ARTIST TIME

YOU'VE heard of flow, right? Athletes talk about getting in the zone, the flow, where time and space seem to disappear. At one point I was training to swim from Alcatraz. Yes, crazy, I know. I was approaching 60 when I decided to start this training. My plan was to complete the Alcatraz swim before my 60th birthday. Unfortunately I got sidelined by two shoulder injuries and didn't get to complete the Alcatraz swim. But for the two years I was training I would regularly experience flow in the swimming pool. I swam at night in an outdoor pool. Winter and summer, didn't matter. I started with five laps, then ten, then twenty, then twenty-five.

There would come a time, every night, when I was swimming that I would swear to you I could breathe underwater. I could swim forever. It was flow. It was the most blissful feeling I have ever experienced outside of my studio.

I'm thinking about training for the Alcatraz swim again. I miss that

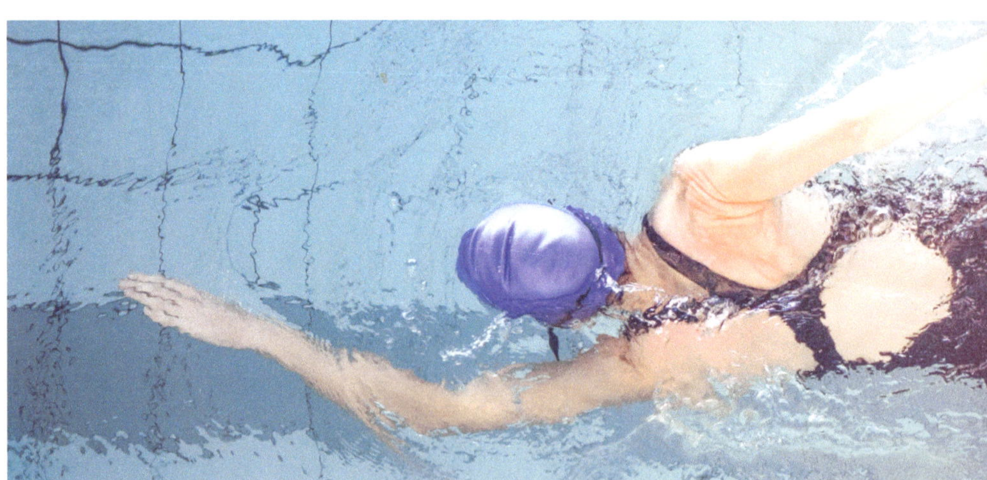

feeling of flow while being in the water. Now I may never complete the Alcatraz swim, but I can have flow anyway. All I have to do is swim with no expectations.

I experience flow on a regular basis in the studio. There's an almost trance-like state that happens when I'm working on a painting. Time seems to stand still. I forget to eat. I don't feel pain. It doesn't take long for this magical state to show up, either. I don't have to work for hours to access this timeless state, what I call the "bliss bubble". It happens quite quickly when I start working.

My point in sharing this is that you don't have to have a big fancy studio or work for hours and hours to get into this cool, flow state.

Robert Motherwell, the famous American artist, was once asked how long it took him to paint one of the large paintings, 8 feet by 12 feet, in the series "Elegy to the Spanish Republic." He is said to have replied "twenty years and twenty minutes." Implying that it took

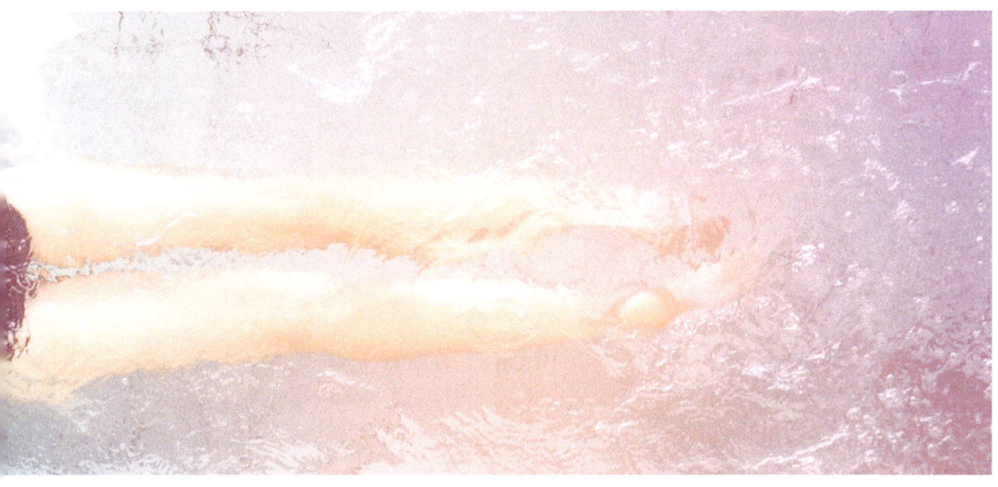

him twenty years to be prepared to paint it, and twenty minutes to get the paint down on the canvas.

Artists work in a special space-time continuum. Einstein knew about this kind of time. He called it the Theory of Relativity. I call it Artist Time.

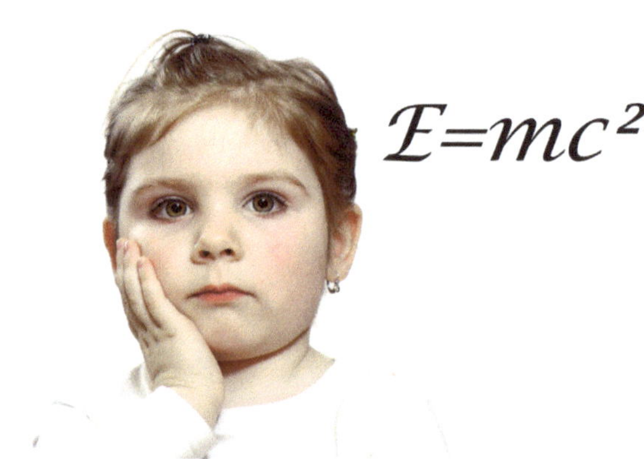

Let's look at Artist Time and the idea that time does not equal value in art.

What do I mean by this?

If you create something and it's wonderful, it does not matter how long it took you to make it.

The only thing that matters is that you love it and it feels true.

I've been teaching painting for over 25 years. I've looked at thousands of paintings by hundreds of students and I can tell you

this for sure - time does not equal value in art. I've seen paintings
created in ten minutes that knocked my socks off. And I've seen
a student labor and labor over a painting, hour upon hour, only to
come up with a heavy, uninspired result.

What gives? Is this some kind of cosmic joke? You work and work,
hone your skills, learn to be disciplined only to have your best work
happen in ten minutes while you're cleaning your brushes on the
canvas?

I wish I had a hard and fast answer for you but I don't. I only know
that there is some magical, mystical thing that happens sometimes
and the painting or drawing or poem falls down from the ether
whole cloth. Finished without a hair out of place.

This is why you must work like a major league baseball player.
See the chapter "You Should Make Art Like Barry Bonds Played
Baseball." Because you never know when this magical thing is
going to happen. So you get into the batter's box every time.
You become a working artist. You go to work in the studio/
kitchen/spare bedroom and you make something. You make ten
somethings hoping that the magic will fall down onto your table.

Listen, I am the first one to say that there are no magic painting
fairies that will delight you with otherworldly inspiration if you
sit and stare are your navel long enough. Nope. That is not the
way. But I will tell you this: I believe you can coax whatever
magical thingie this is, onto your canvas by just working. Seriously,

just pushing paint around on the canvas without any ideas or expectations and suddenly that voodoo is the voodoo you do so well.

And by working I also mean taking a break. What? Yes, taking a break is part of the work. I know this seems like a paradox but stay with me. The not-working part is as important as the working part. This creating thing is not linear. It's furtive. It's like trying to take a picture of your cat. You can't get a good picture of the cat because it's so aware of the camera. So you have to pretend you're NOT taking a picture of the cat to get a good one. With making art, you have to pretend you don't want to be inspired.

Inspiration, The Big Momma Muse, is fussy. She's shy. She wants to be courted.

In her book "Big Magic", Elizabeth Gilbert talks about this at length. The idea of coaxing Inspiration into the room. She even talks about dressing up for Inspiration. Putting on lipstick and washing her face. I sweep the studio floor as a sort of ritual when I'm coming

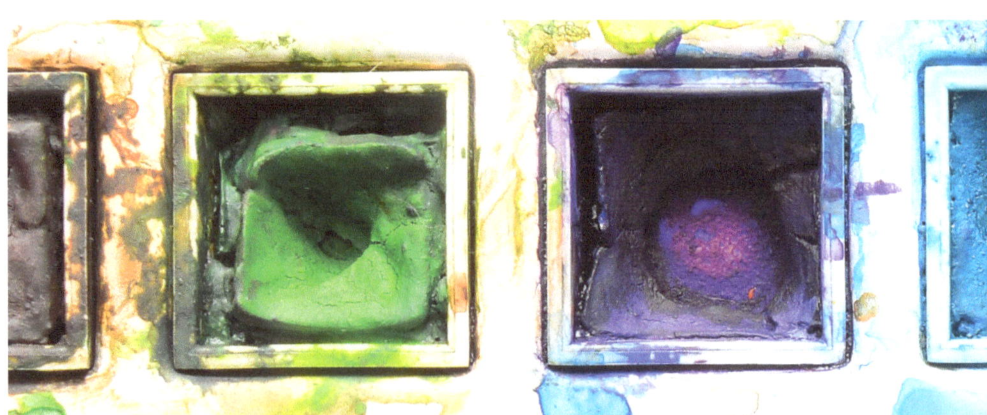

back from traveling or if I'm starting a new series. Other artists or writers take showers, garden or run on the beach.

The trick here is to just act as if. As if you are inspired and you know what you're doing. Don't whine about not being inspired. Just push some paint around or scratch a few lines on paper and see what happens.

Honestly, Elizabeth Gilbert named her book correctly. "Big Magic" is the truth. It is magic, but it's also NOT magic. If you can just hold that paradox in your head and heart while you putter around you'll be fine.

And remember, never point the camera directly at the cat. And never point yourself right at the Big Momma Muse. Sidle up to her, give her a wink and a hug and she'll hang out with you.

Go push some paint around and see what happens.

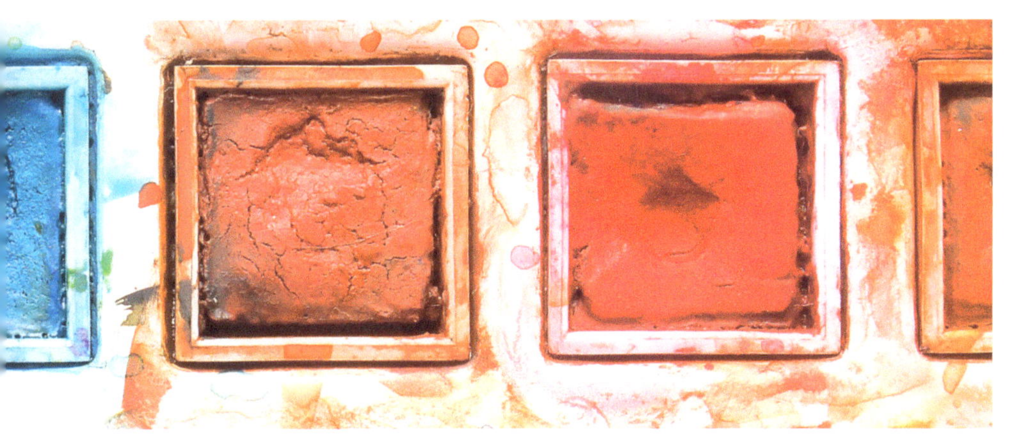

"PERSEVERANCE IS FAILING 19 TIMES AND
SUCCEEDING THE 20TH."

JULIE ANDREWS

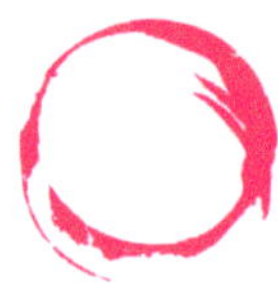

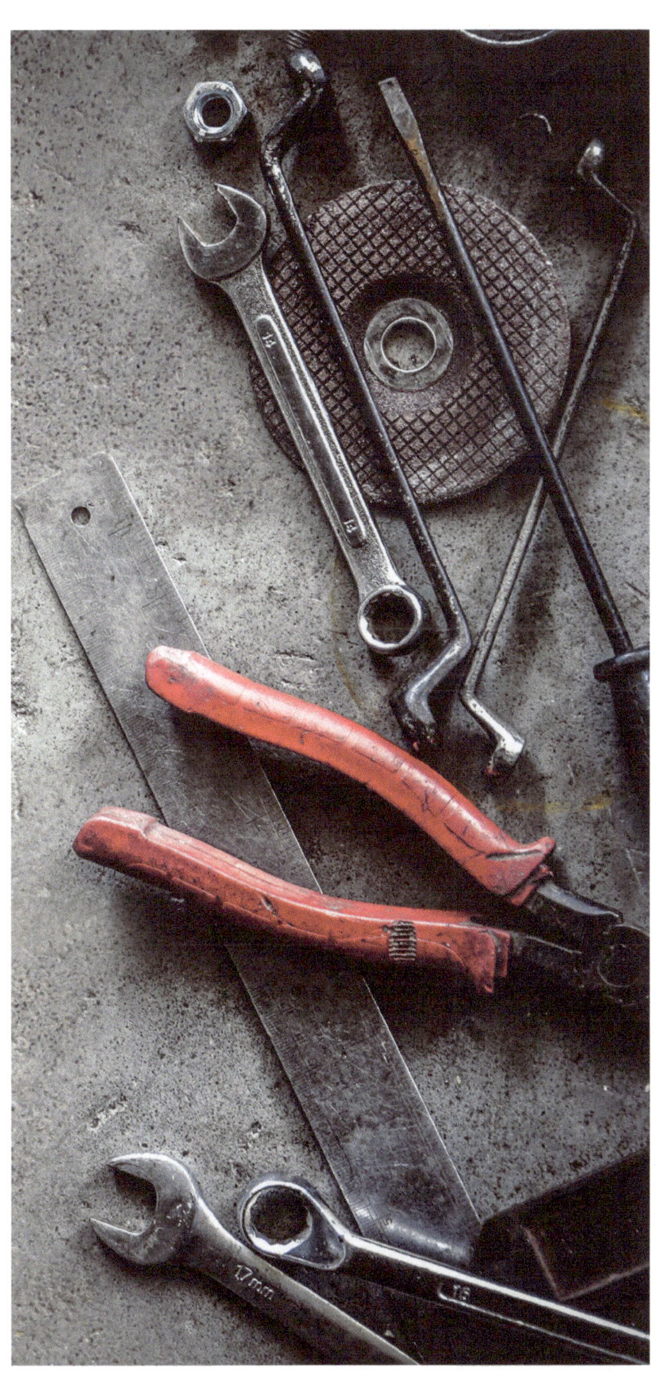

DON'T QUIT YOUR DAY JOB

BORN and raised in India, Vinay Sharma moved to Sacramento from New York City after graduating from Columbia University with a Masters in Computer Engineering.

A few years ago, Vinay came to one of the lectures I regularly do for Golden Artist Colors™. Afterwards he asked me about classes and ended up studying with me. He has gone on to become an extraordinary printmaker, selling and showing his work and even being included in prestigious print journals.

This all happened in about five years.

Oh and by the way, he works full time as a hardware engineer.

He has a passion for creating. He finds the time to create even with a full-time, very demanding job.

Once you get past the idea that you have to have the big studio or forty hours a week to paint or any of those other Artist Myths - then it's pretty easy to find time to create. Ten minutes while the pasta is cooking. Easy, peasy.

The amazing printmaker Kathe Kollwitz created stunning, heart-wrenching prints while she was stirring the soup and had a baby on her hip.

The chameleon-like writer and actor, Tyler Perry, lived in his car off
and on for six years while he was trying to get his first play staged.

Vermeer specialized in domestic scenes. Perhaps because he was
an innkeeper as well as a painter. He reportedly only created thirty-
four paintings in his lifetime.

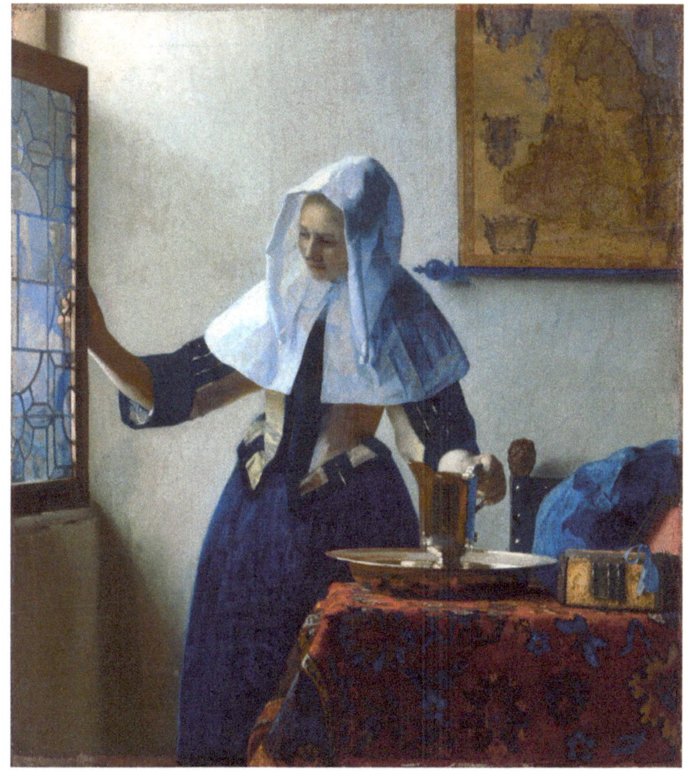

Johannes Vermeer, "Young Woman with a Water
Pitcher", oil on canvas circa 1662

*"We do not need magic to
change the world, we carry
all the power we need inside
ourselves already: we have the
power to imagine better."*
J.K. Rowling

Vincent van Gogh started out as a preacher and painted on the side before managing to get a small allowance from his brother so that he could paint full time.

Joseph Cornell was the full-time caregiver for his brother who had cerebral palsy.

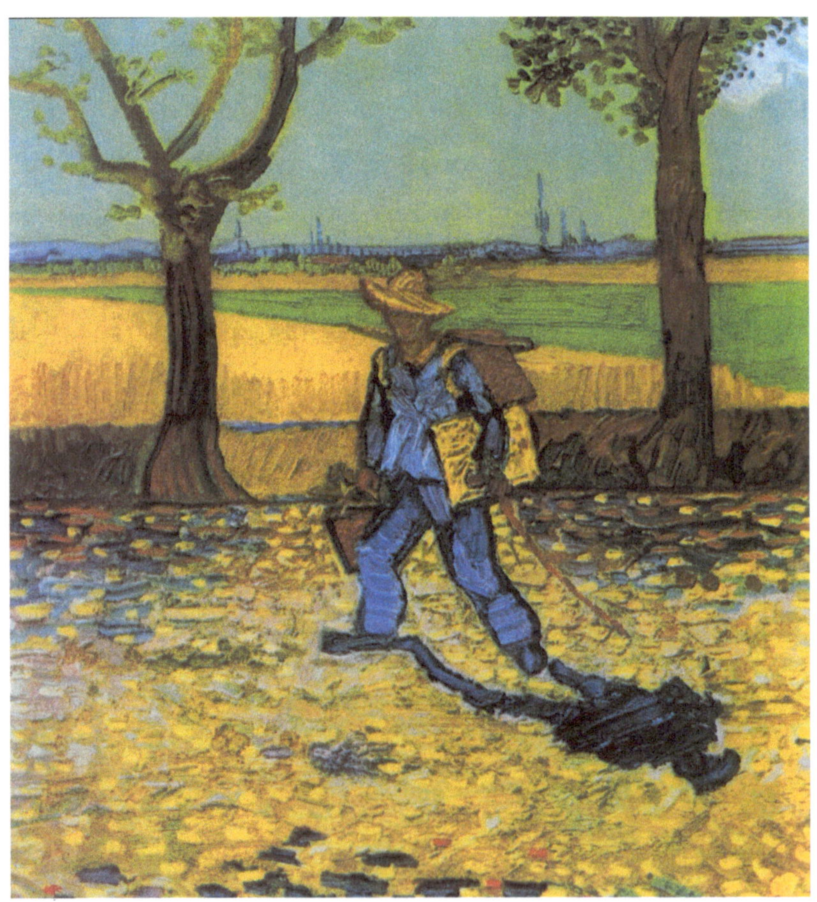

Vincent van Gogh „The Painter on His Way To Work",
oil on canvas, 1888

John Updike, the great American writer, gives young writers advice
to try to write just an hour a day. "Some very good things have
been written in an hour a day."

Think back to something you really wanted. What did you have
to sacrifice in order to obtain it? Maybe it was a kitchen remodel.
You gave up going out to eat for an entire year to get that new Wolf
range. Or maybe it was a gorgeous pair of shoes and you gave up
large café lattés for a month.

What are you willing to sacrifice in order to create art?

A couple of hours of sleep?

A night out with friends?

A two-week vacation?

You can create and have a full-time job. People do it all the time.

Try setting aside just two or three hours a week to make something.
See where it takes you. You may be surprised that the next vacation
you take is to an artist's retreat. Or you may find that it doesn't
feel like sacrifice at all. You may find that you are not only willing,
but anxious to give up a couple hours of sleep to get that collage
finished.

Make it happen. Make it work. Just make stuff.

"I have had my studio practice in Sacramento, CA since 2013 and it has been a very interesting journey for me. There are good studio days and then there are bad studio days. Sometimes it's "Why am I doing this?" and sometimes it's "Whoa! I am on fire!" The key is to remember that creativity comes in bursts. Yes, it is hard at times with a full time job. Your job can take a lot of your time and energy. It may eat into your studio time but at the end of the day it is your choice to define the boundaries and make the time. I enjoy working as an engineer and as an artist. For me it is a balancing act. I have done shows, commissions and have curated and juried shows while having my full time job as an engineer. Many times I have struggled with long hours and the pressure of a full-time job causing my art career to take a back seat - but there is always a way to make it work and strike a good balance. Time management and organizing your day to day life will help strike a balance. So you can can have both! A full time job and an art career."

-Vinay Sharma

""There is no must in art because art is free."
Wassily Kandinsky

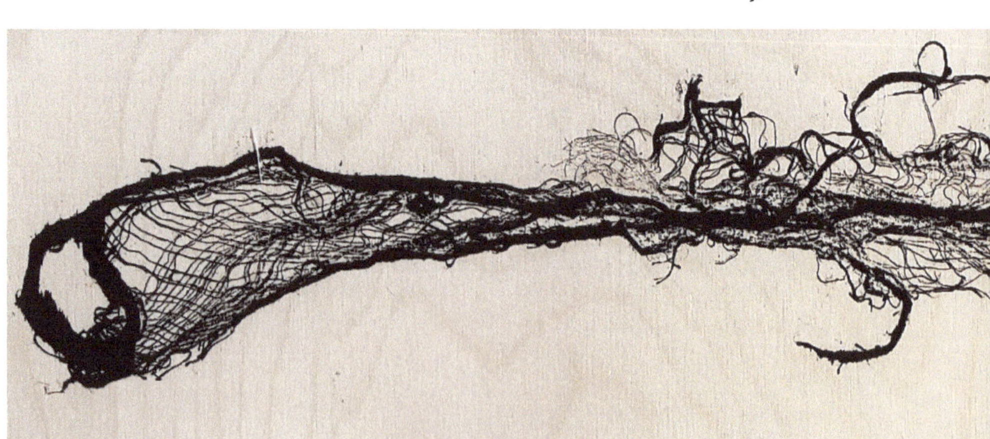

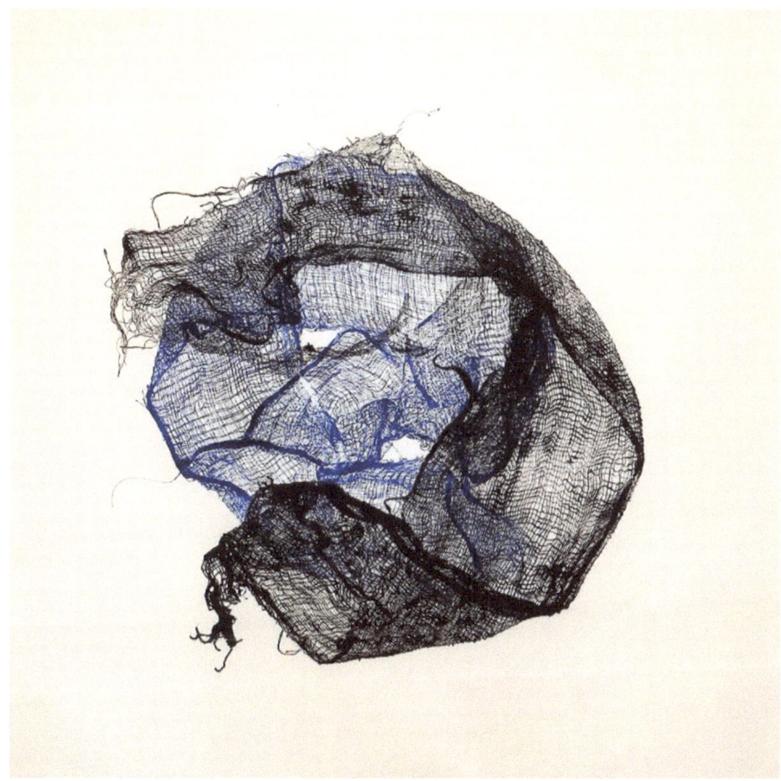

Vinay Sharma "Untitled #7" , monotype on birch panel, 18" x 18" 2018.

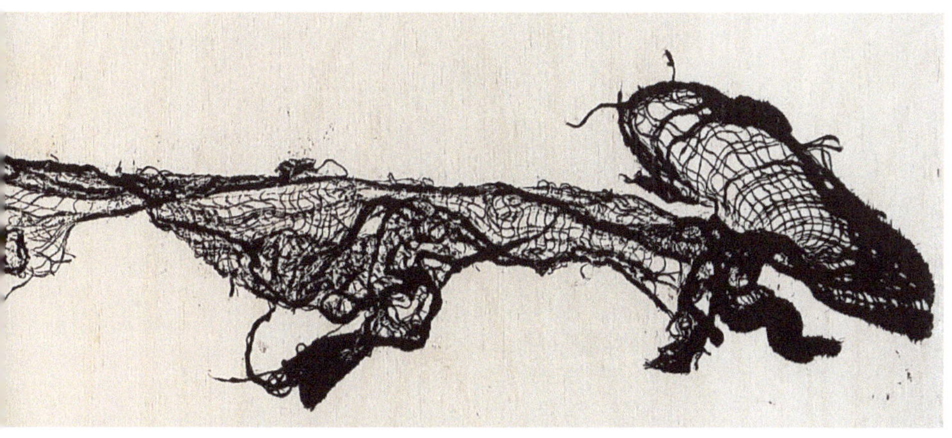

Vinay Sharma "Untitled #5" , monotype on birch panel, 24" x 6", 2018

"Do small things with great love."

Mother Theresa

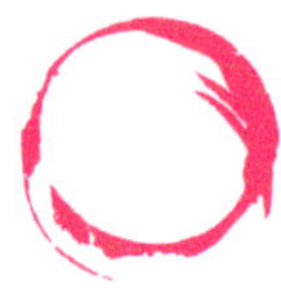

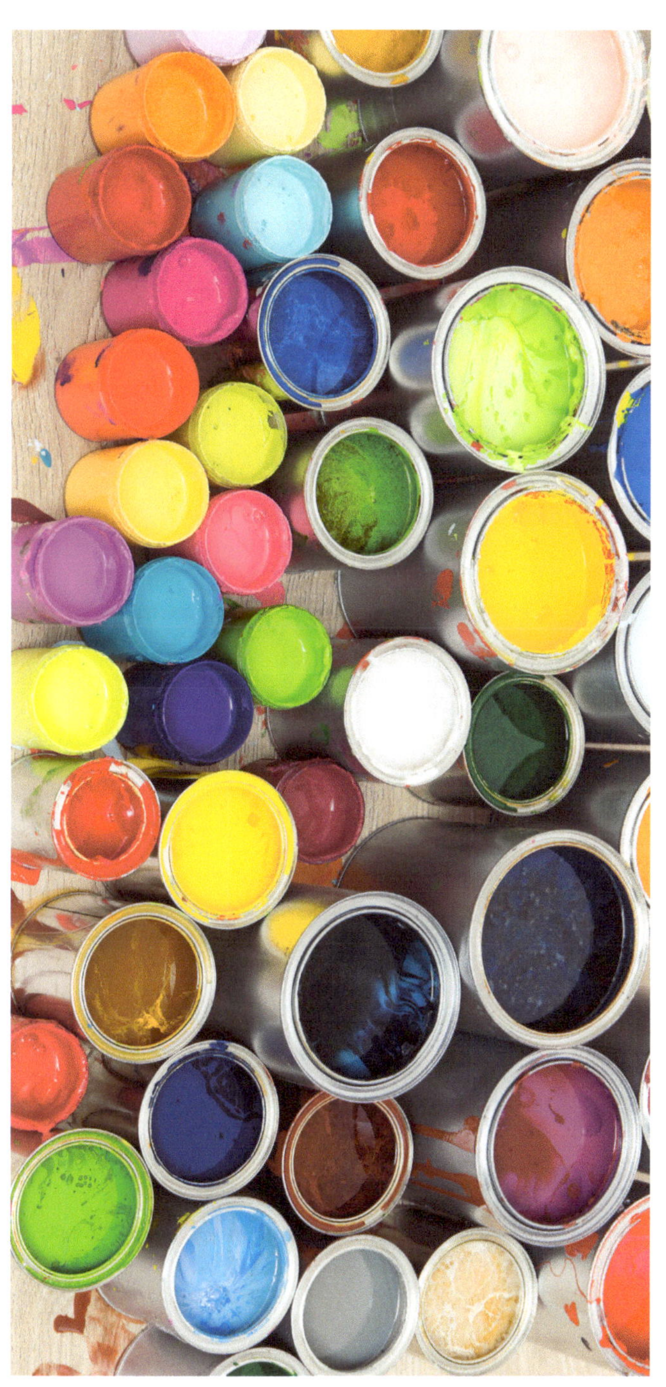

CHAPTER TEN

SIZE DOESN'T MATTER

MY pal, Robert Jean Ray, creates provocative and very interesting collages that are about the size of a postage stamp. Recently he branched out into large format collage going up to a whopping five by seven inches. Wow. His entire catalogue of work fits neatly into a shoebox. He can work anywhere. He's had gallery and museum shows. His work is widely collected.

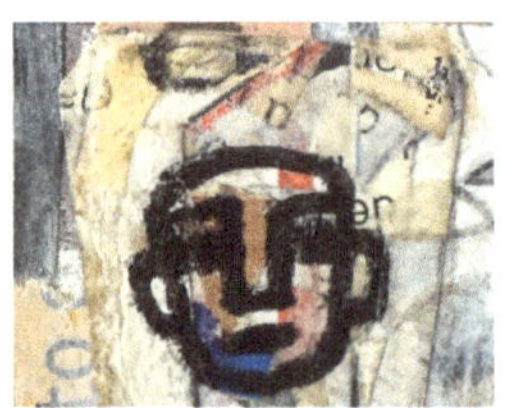 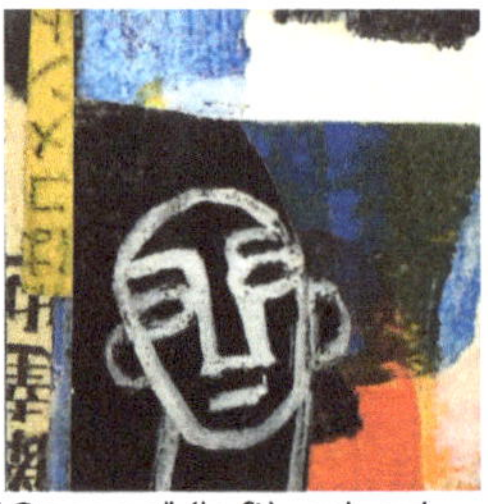

Robert Jean Ray "Change of Season" (left), mixed media collage, "Studio Portrait #9" (right), collage. Shown actual size.

Ray merges linear depictions of the human with collage compositions inspired by urban street graphics. Influenced by 20th century German and Italian expressionism, his work consists primarily of diminutively sized artwork with a strong visual impact.

Think you need to work large to make an impact? Think again.

Joseph Cornell made wonderful assemblage creations, usually about the size of a cigar box. In fact, some of them were made inside a cigar box.

And speaking of cigar boxes, the great American painter, Richard Diebenkorn did an entire series of paintings on cigar box lids and gave them to his friends for Christmas presents. Oh to be on his Christmas list! If you look at the cigar box paintings online or in a book, you can't tell them apart from his very large paintings from the same series "Ocean Park." The quality of the paint and composition is the same no matter how small or large the painting.

The point here is that size does not matter.

This is an obstacle we use when we are procrastinating.

"I don't have a big studio so I can't make art."

"I'll make a mess so I can't paint here."

"If it's small it's not important."

"It has to be big to express my ideas."

"Creativity is allowing yourself to make mistakes. Art is knowing which ones to keep."
Scott Adams

These are all obstacles that Procrastination will throw at you to keep you from working.

Don't fall for it. Just get out that tiny paper and start gluing things to it.

Jess Collins or "Jess" as he was known, was a collage artist who lived and worked in San Francisco from the 1940s to his death in 2004. Check out his amazing "paste-ups" online. All created with just scissors and magazines. Some of them are just eight by ten inches.

The work you do doesn't depend on the size. The work you do depends on an authentic expression of your inspiration.

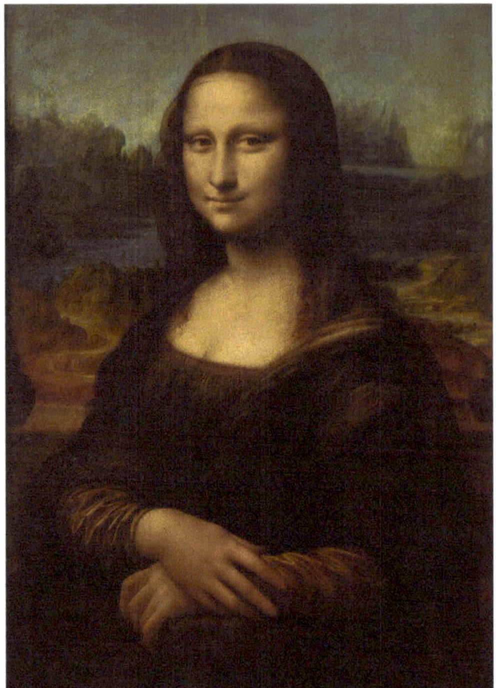

Leonardo da Vinci "Mona Lisa"
Oil on Poplar Wood 1503-06

Just do the work and put it out there. You never know what's going to appeal to someone.

Of course, everyone knows the Mona Lisa is only 21 inches by 30 inches.

Many years ago, when I was just beginning my career, I did outdoor shows with the San Francisco Artist Guild. Yep, I sold my work right off the sidewalk. The Guild has been around for 50 or so years and is the oldest outdoor art group in San Francisco. It's a great way to gain exposure for your work, meet like-minded artists and get a feel for what it's like to be a working artist when you're just starting out.

At one of the shows I did in Union Square a woman came over, went right past my big important pieces, took my smallest piece off of the exhibit and clutched it to her chest. It was a mixed media piece that I had put out just as "filler" for the other artwork. It was an okay piece, not my best work, just okay. But I needed to pad

the exhibit a little so I hung it with the "best" pieces. The woman
hugged it to her chest and because she didn't speak English could
only say "Visa?" Ahh, the international language of credit cards.
I said yes and made the sale. I thanked her and she went away
hugging the wrapped artwork, a big smile on her face. That was the
only sale I made that day.

If I had decided that that small mixed media piece was not good
enough, or big enough, to hang with my other, better pieces (or
what I had decided were my "better" pieces) I would have gone
home that day without making a sale.

Don't make decisions about what you make after it's finished.
Sure, make design decisions and color decisions and all the other
decisions you need to make while you're creating it. But once
it's finished, put it out there and leave it alone. Big, small or in-
between, the artwork no longer belongs to you. It belongs to the
Universe.

The work will find its home. Just trust it.

Trust your Inspiration and find your people.

Leave the rest up to this thing we call Creativity.

"I REALLY BELIEVE THAT IF YOU PRACTICE ENOUGH
YOU COULD PAINT THE 'MONA LISA' WITH A
TWO-INCH BRUSH."

BOB ROSS

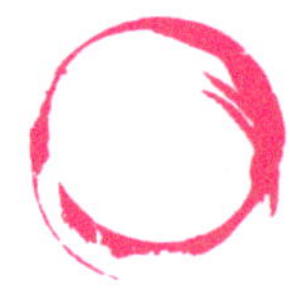

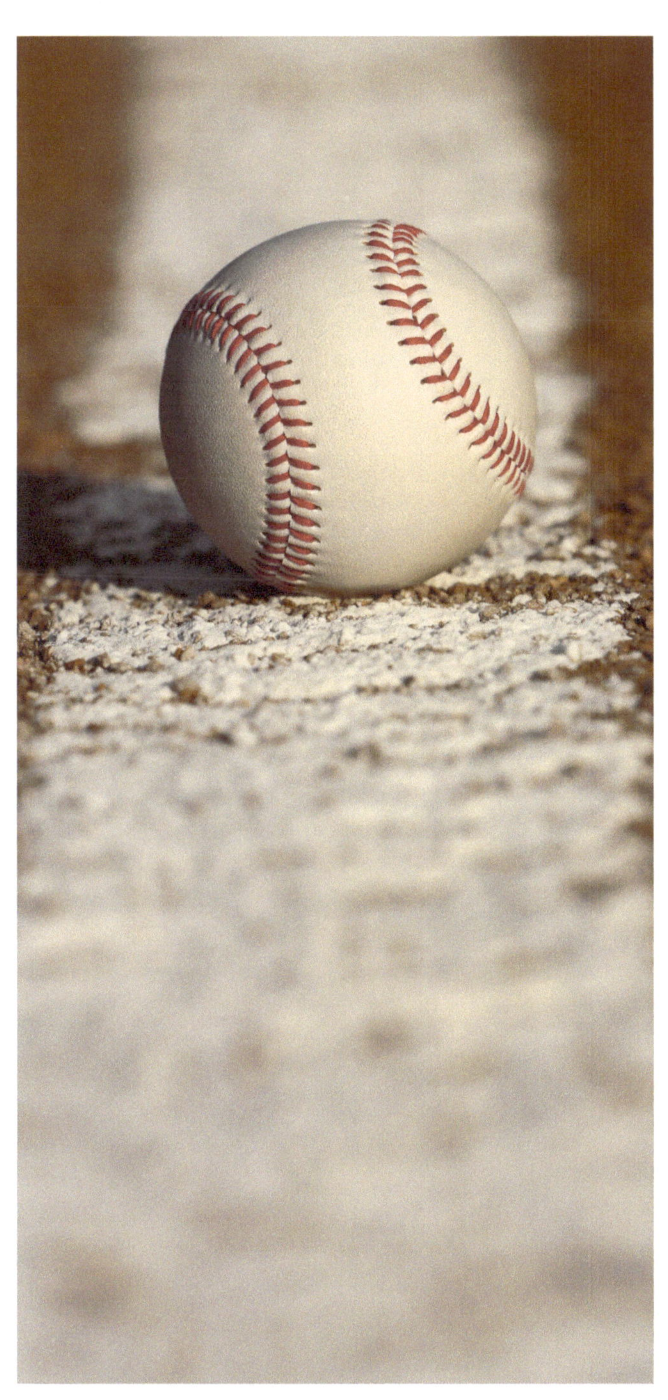

Chapter Eleven

You Should Make Art Like Barry Bonds Played Baseball

WE are big San Francisco Giants fans at our house. I've been to many, many major league baseball games. One thing I've noticed - all of the ball players take batting practice. I don't care if they're hitting 350 or 120. They all get out there and practice.

And they strike out. The big bats like Barry Bonds strike out. But they also get on base. They get doubles or triples. And they all practice at the beginning of the game. Just to stay loose. Just to get the bat warmed up.

Now whether or not you like Barry Bonds is beside the point. Whether you think he was "juicing" during his career does not matter.

What matters is that he practiced. Over and over again. Even after he broke home run records. I saw him hit home run number 720,

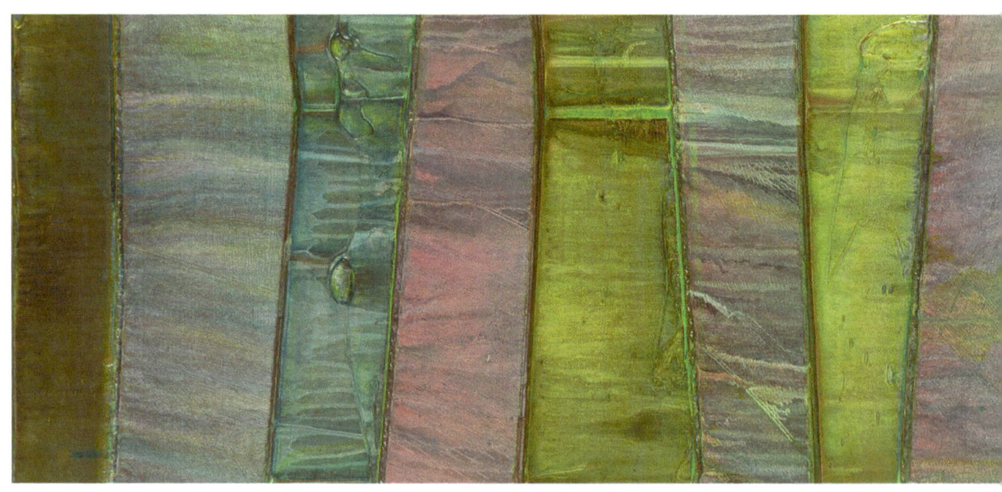

I think it was. But I also saw him strike out. I saw him fly out to right field.

How does all this relate to making art? Well you gotta get in the batter's box to even strike out. You have to make something, anything, to get to the next something. The first one may be lousy or just okay. The second, third, twentieth, may be lousy or okay. But somewhere along the way, you're going to hit a grand slam homer.

The Muse is going to land on your shoulder (you won't even feel it) and BAM something magical will happen to the drawing/painting/ collage/sculpture you're working on. When this happens you had better sit up and take notice. The Big Momma Muse has just paid you a visit. You take that nugget and work with it, cradle it, cherish it. It will serve you well.

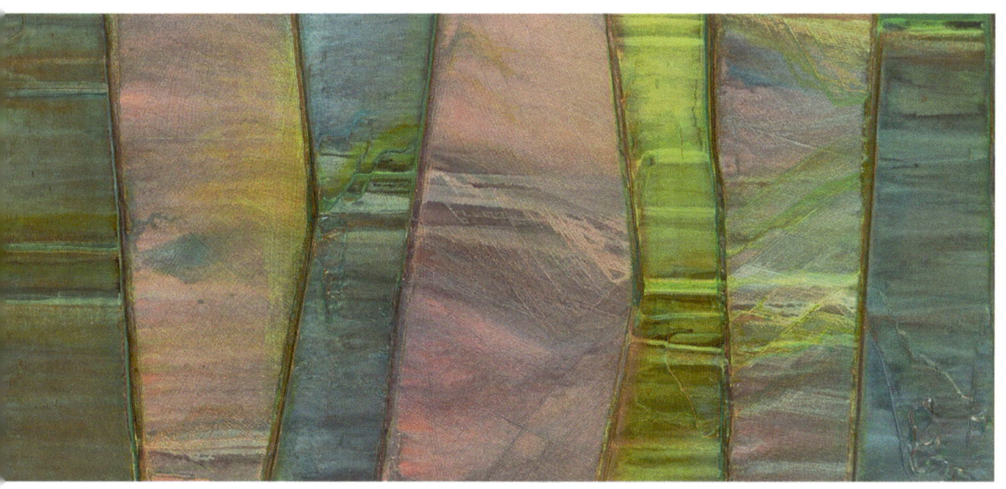

Juan Alonso Rodriguez "Llano" (detail)

Here's how to take advantage of this inspirational moment. Once you get the "aha" moment out of the way and you've come back to Earth, take a minute to examine what you've done. Try to be objective and reverse engineer what happened. Don't worry – this is not going to take the magic away. It's going to make it possible for you to recreate the magic.

Ask yourself some questions about how you created this wonderful thing. Go back in your mind and remember all the steps you took to get to the end result. Write down the steps. Be as detailed as possible. The important thing is that you recreate the steps for yourself.

Believe me, you know how this magical artwork was created. You created it! I cannot count how many times I have stood at the easel of a student and said, "So how did you do this part here?" and the answer I get is "I don't know." Once again, there are no magical painting fairies folks! You did this. You created it. You get to take credit for it.

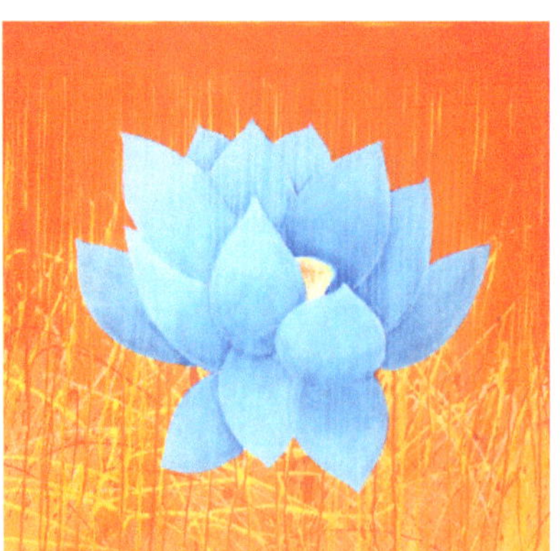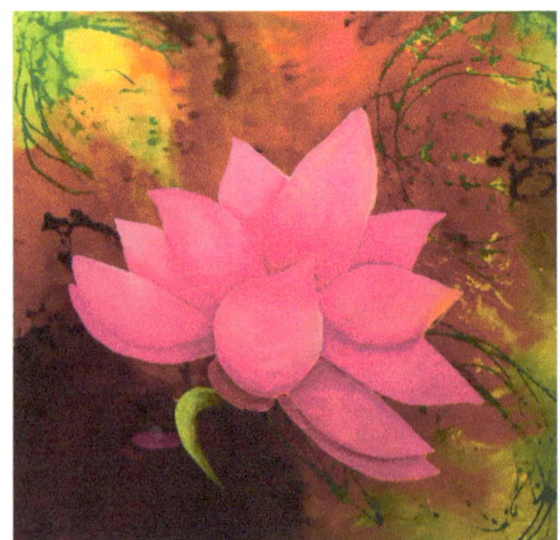

Tesia Blackburn, "Blue Lotus" (left), "Ambuja" (right), acrylic on canvas 72" x 72"

Just be patient with yourself and really dig in and look at the artwork. Tell yourself about the artwork and how it was created as if you are explaining it to a child. I talk to myself all the time. It's a really good thing there isn't a webcam in the studio. I must look and sound kinda crazy. I actually talk to myself in the third person as in "geez Tesia, why did you put that blue there?" It works for me and they haven't hauled me away to the loony bin just yet.

Once you've identified how you made the artwork, start another painting/drawing/sculpture based on the first one. Don't copy it – just refer to it. Using the first painting as inspiration, carry elements from it to all of the other canvases. Before you know it, you will have created a series. The art will have a synergy and each piece will relate to the others in the series.

I always work in series. One good idea can keep me going over fifty or sixty pieces. And I'm not the only artist who works this way. Wassily Kandinsky, Picasso, Stuart Davis, Lee Krasner and a host of other artists worked in series.

"And the day came when the risk to remain tight in a bud was more painful than the risk it took to blossom."
Anaïs Nin

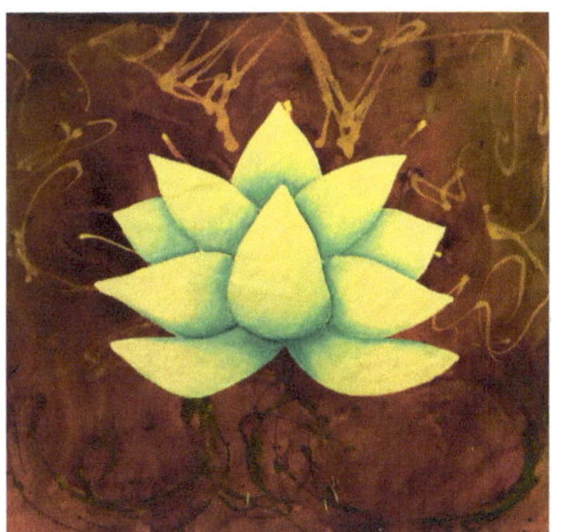 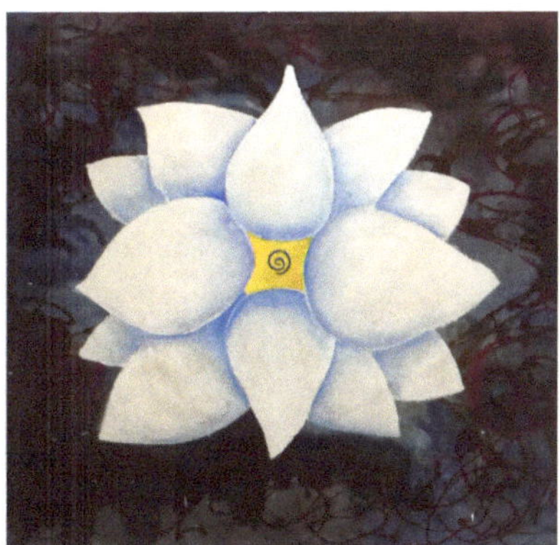

Tesia Blackburn, "Neeraja" (left), "Padma" (right) acrylic on canvas 72" x 86"

Don't worry if the second, third or fifth aren't as good as the first one, just soldier on. Practice, practice, practice. Keep making them; you may have to make twenty to get ten good ones. But that's not bad. Damn, those are good odds in Vegas!

It's like a dance. Maybe it's a color and a shape from the first painting. That blue and that funny shape with the pointy edges. Start there. Get something down on the second canvas or paper that you had in the first painting. Start moving stuff around and see what happens. The stars may line up and you'll make the magic.

But remember even major league ball players strike out.

Just get in the batter's box and start swinging.

Sooner or later you'll hit it out of the park.

THE STRATA SERIES

One of my favorite artists, Juan Alonso of Seattle works in series. Cuban-born Juan Alonso-Rodríguez is an award winning, self-taught artist with a career spanning over three decades. His work is in many private and public collections including Microsoft, General Mills, Tacoma Art Museum and Portland Art Museum. Besides making studio work, he has also created several permanent, site-specific, public works in the Pacific Northwest.

"Working in series, I can explore a concept or theme until it has little left to reveal. At times it helps to create parameters, as in use of form, composition or color in order to concentrate on message. My full body of work consists of several series, one generally inspired or sparked by the culmination of the previous one. The series are related but can stand alone.

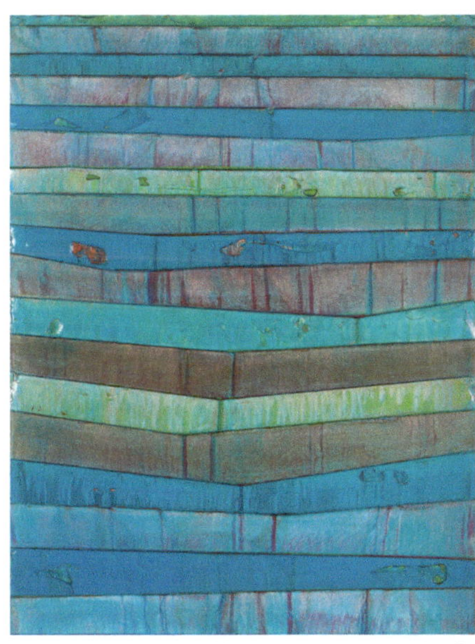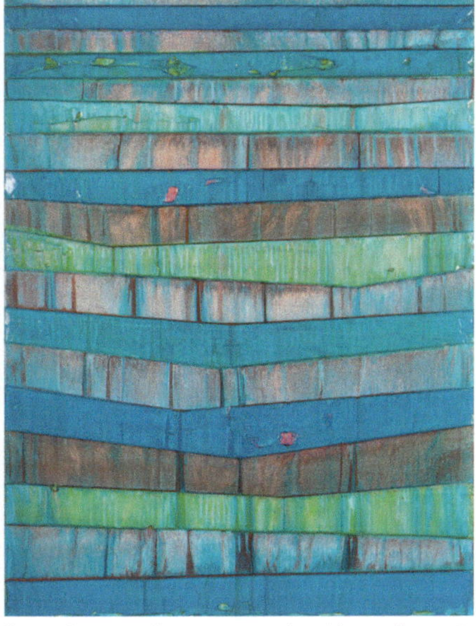

Juan Alonso Rodriguez "Aquamarine" , diptych, acrylic on panel, 48" x 74" 2018

The Strata series is based on both the literal and figurative meanings of the word. There are physical layers on these paintings. Alternating, slightly raised horizontal bands are created using moulding paste, and the paintings' depth of color is achieved by using sometimes up to twenty-five layers of diluted, translucent acrylics. Four coats of UVLS polymer varnish both protect and seal the work but also bring out some of the earlier laid colors, creating subtle contrasts and effects that evoke veined marble.

*Figuratively, the layers speak to our own planet's shifts and constant
evolution. Iridescent paints remind us of metals we mine to create
our own structures and the multi-leveled compositions refer to the
relationship between the man-made and the natural environment.
There are architectural elements to these works: We have been digging
to create foundations and building level structures on precarious and
uneven ground for as long as we have been constructing shelter.*

*In my opinion, the most successful structures are those that are
built to blend in or compliment their environment and to be able to
maintain aesthetic integrity as they weather over time.
The Strata paintings are inspired by the concept of structures
referencing and evoking nature."*

- Juan Alonso

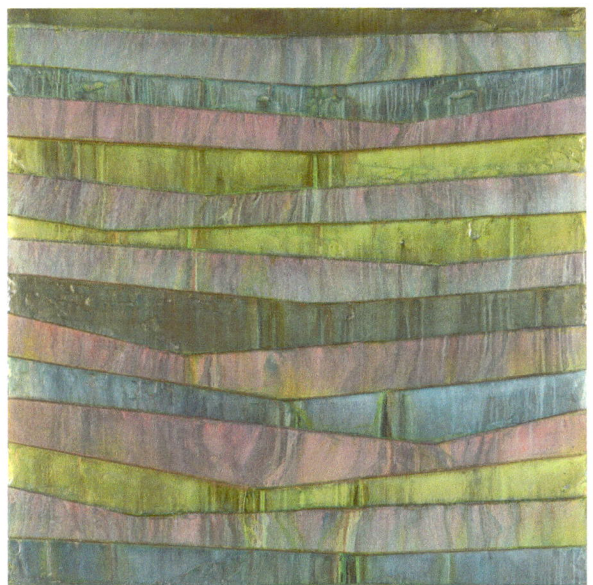
Juan Alonso Rodriguez "Llano",
acrylic on panel, 48" x 48" 2018

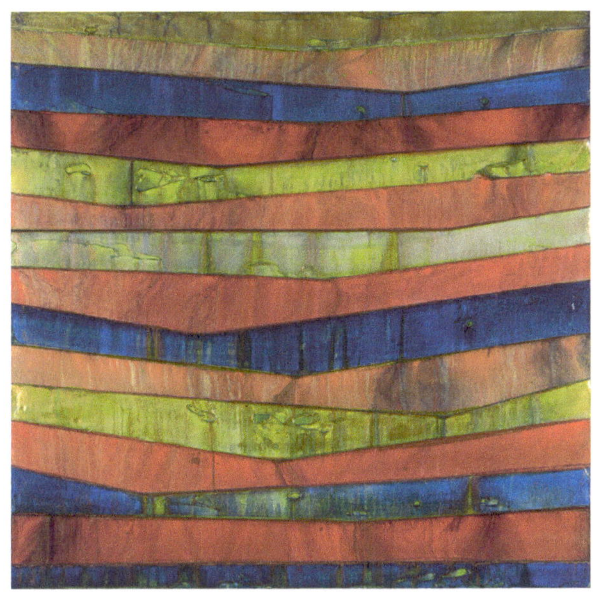
Juan Alonso Rodriguez "Crepuscúlo",
acrylic on panel, 48" x 48" 2018

You see, I told you there would be contradictions, repetitions and adult language. I hope you've found my thoughts and opinions useful. And remember, these are just that, my thoughts and opinions. If you stop ten people on the street, at least five of them are likely to disagree with me. Clearly those people are not my tribe. That's why it's important to find your people.

If you are already in my tribe (and you know who you are) you know how much I love you.

YOU are the reason I get up in the morning.
YOU lift me up.
YOU make me laugh.
YOU bring tears to my eyes with your courage and creativity.

If you're just joining, welcome to the party.

It's a real lovefest in here.

Jesia

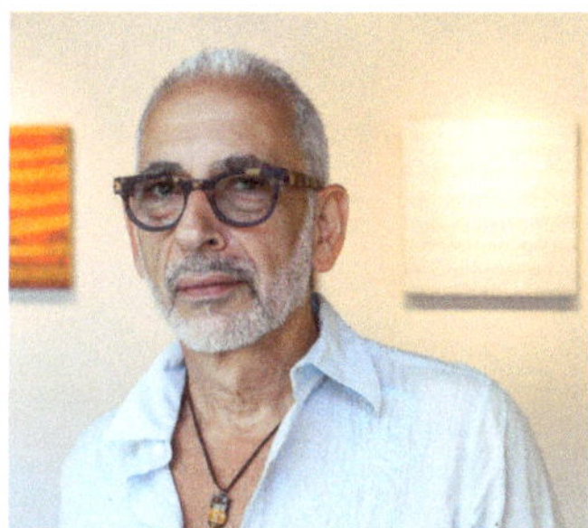

Juan Alonso Rodriguez
Seattle, WA
JuanAlonsoStudio.com

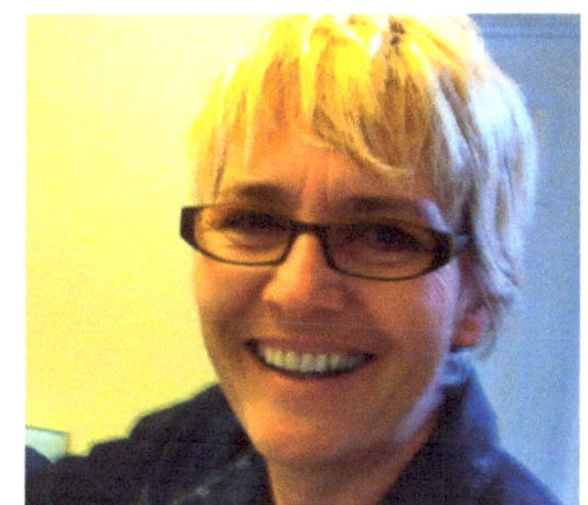

Tina Pressler
San Francisco Bay Area
TinaPressler.com

*"The most courageous act
is still to think for
yourself. Aloud."
Coco Chanel*

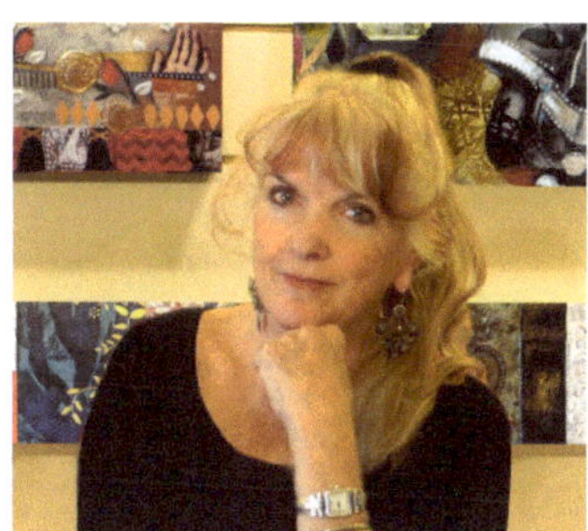

Darlene McElroy
Santa Fe, NM
DarleneOliviaMcelroy.com

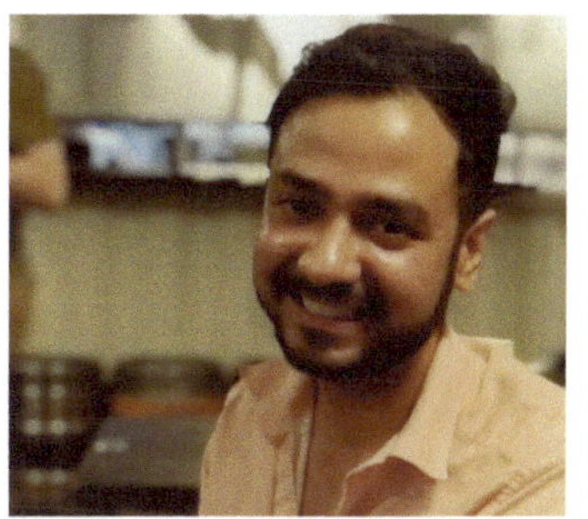

Vinay Sharma
Sacramento, CA
ArthouseOnR.com

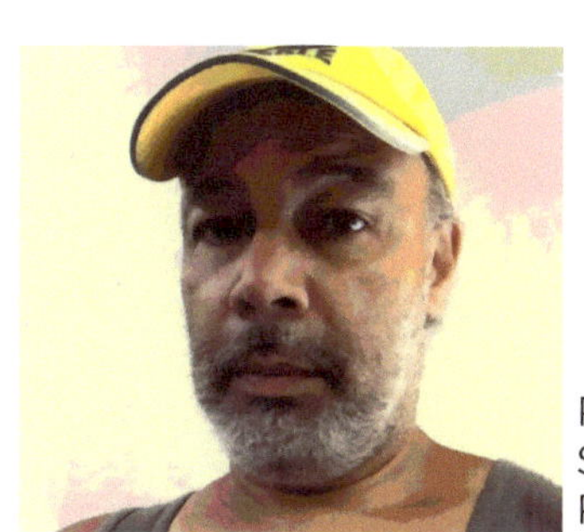

Robert Jean Ray
Sacramento, CA
RobertMicroRay@gmail.com

"BE KIND WHENEVER POSSIBLE.
IT IS ALWAYS POSSIBLE."

DALAI LAMA

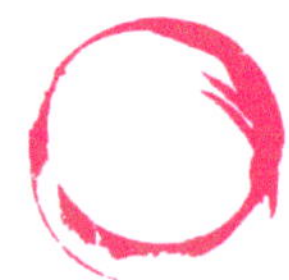

About the Editor

Patrice Drago is an East Coast abstract artist and arts writer, and is an Artist in Residence at Maryland Hall for the Creative Arts. During her professional career in the hospitality industry, she used her creative writing, investigative and artistic skills to create in-depth training programs and brand materials, write video scripts, simulations, and user-friendly training, editing the writing of numerous developers. She is an arts columnist for the Annapolis Capital Gazette in Maryland, an arts blogger for the area's destination marketing organization, Visit Annapolis, and is the Board VP of Public Relations and Communications Chair for Maryland Federation of Art, a nation-wide non-profit art organization of 700+ members.

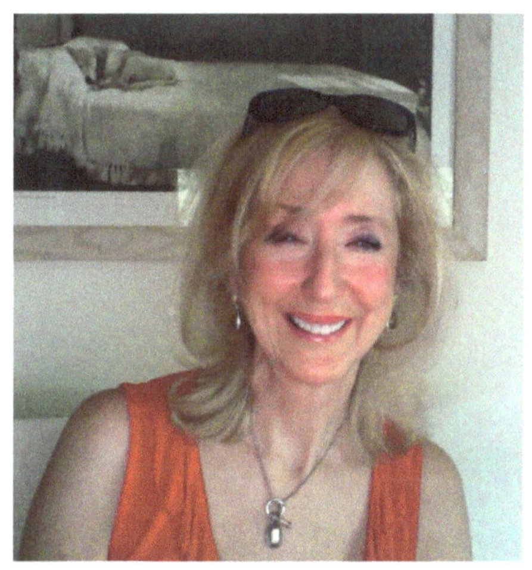

PatriceDrago.com

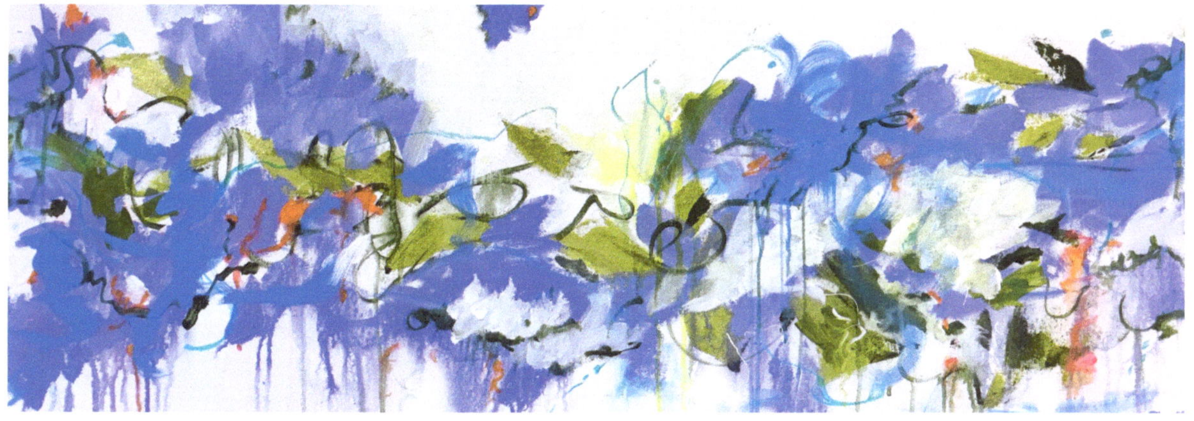

Patrice Drago "Floating" 16" x 40" Acrylic on Canvas

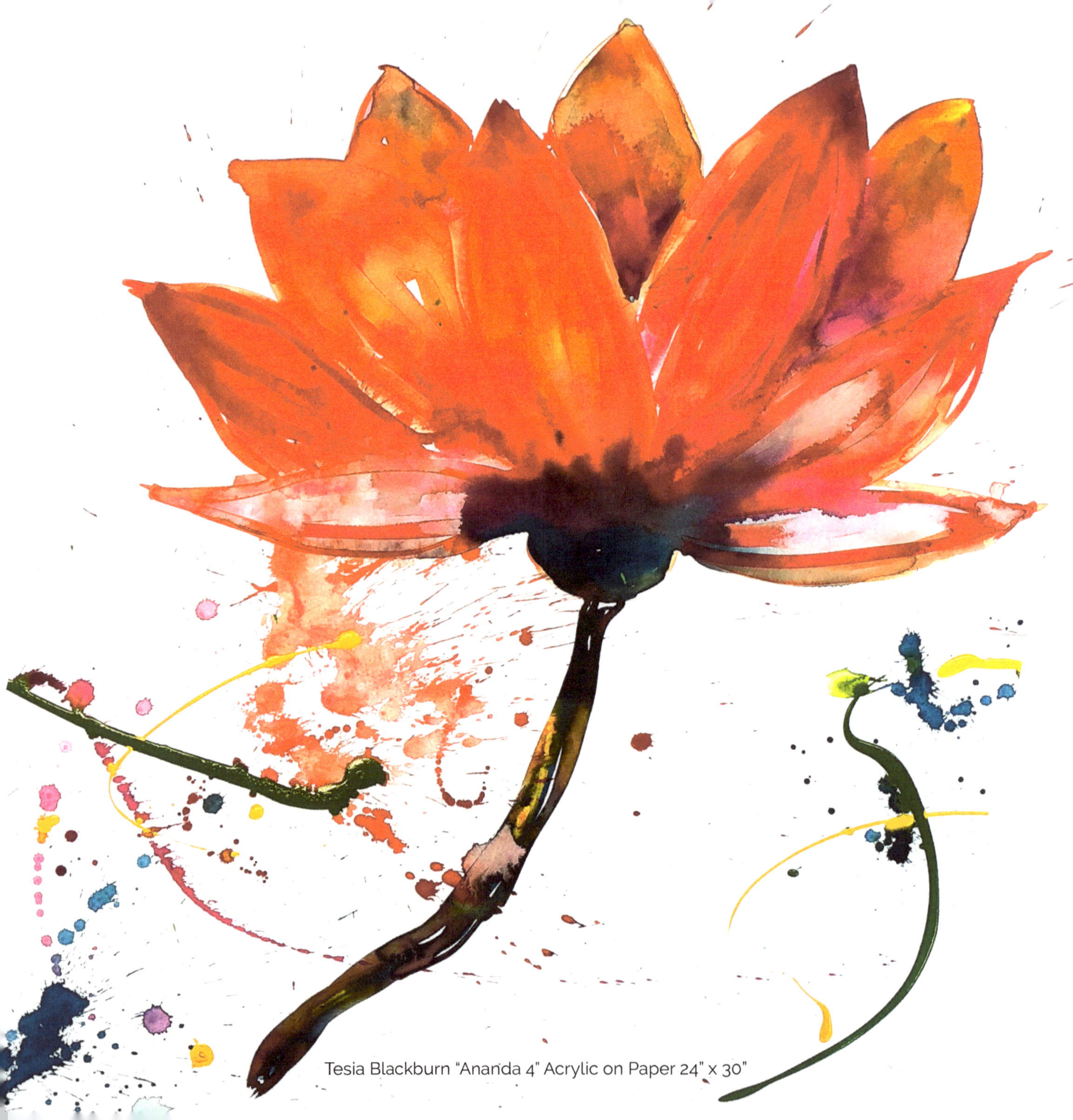

Tesia Blackburn "Ananda 4" Acrylic on Paper 24" x 30"

ABOUT THE AUTHOR

TESIA BLACKBURN has been a working artist and teacher in the San Francisco Bay Area for over 25 years. In 2000 she was hired by Golden Artist Colors™, as the Golden Certified Working Artist in San Francisco. In 2014 her first book "Acrylic Painting with Passion" was published by Northlight Books and is now in its second paperback edition. Her work hangs in homes, offices, hotels and hospitals all over the world.

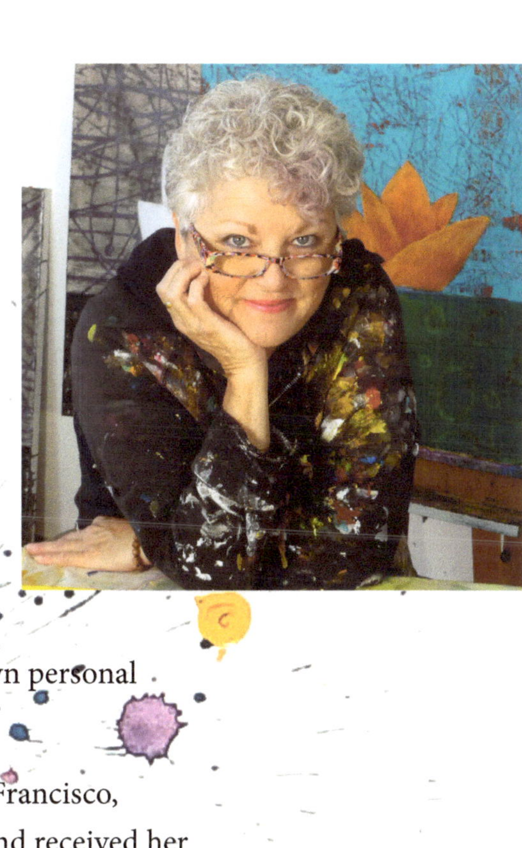

A beloved teacher, Tesia's classes and workshops are often sold out. Whether she's teaching a painting retreat in Santa Fe or a weekly class in San Francisco, her approach is the same; help the student find their own personal voice and express it.

She received her BFA from the Academy of Art in San Francisco, studied lithography at the San Francisco Art Institute and received her Master's of Art from John F. Kennedy University in Orinda, California.

AcrylicDiva.com and BlackburnFineArt.com

PHOTO CREDITS

Every effort has been made to trace the copyright holders and obtain permission to reproduce images. Please contact the publisher with any inquiries or information.

Pages 1-21, 26, 31, 33, 35-36, 39, 42-43, 53, 59, 61, 72-73, 74, 79, 87, 93 Adobe Stock Photos.

Pages 23, 25 Tina Pressler, TinaPressler.com used with permission.

Page 29, 49, 57, 62-63, 65, 76-77, 96-97, 106-7, Tesia Blackburn, AcrylicDiva.com used with permission.

Page 41, Darlene McElroy, DarleneMcElroy.com used with permission.

Page 45, Wassily Kandinsky "Murnau With Church, 1910", by Ermell, licensed under CC by 2.0.

Page 46, Vincent van Gogh, "Self Portrait, 1887", Art Institute of Chicago, licensed under CC by 2.0.

Page 51, Darlene McElroy, used with permission.

Page 55, Stuart Davis, "Lucky Strike 1921", by User: Berichard, licensed under CC by 2.0.

Page 67, Arthur Dove, "Clouds and Water, 1930", Alfred Stieglitz Collection, https://www.metmuseum.org/art/collection/search/488484, licensed under CC by 2.0.

Page 69, Carmen Herrera, "Rondo (Blue and Yellow), 1965", Source: https://flic.kr/p/5vyjn2, Author: https://www.flickr.comphotosnostri-imago, licensed under CC by 2.0.

Page 72, Albert Einstein with his wife, Elsa (cropped), April 2, 1921, Underwood and Underwood, New York, licensed under CC by 2.0.

Page 81, Johannes Vermeer, "Young Woman with a Water Pitcher, circa 1662", Metropolitan Museum of Art, Source: Google Arts and Culture: https://artsandculture.google.com/asset/ogH-Waxey-9HBA, licensed under CC by 2.0.

Page 82, Vincent van Gogh, "The Painter on His Way To Work, July 1888", destroyed. Source: Vincent van Gogh: In der Provence, R.Piper & Co, Verlag, München 1977, ISBN 3492110703, licensed under CC by 2.0.

Page 84-85, Vinay Sharma, arthouseonr.com/artists/vinay-sharma/, used with permission.

Page 88, Robert Jean Ray, robertmicroray@gmail.com, used with permission.

Page 90, Leonardo da Vinci, "La Gioconda (The Mona Lisa), 1503-1505. Current location: Louvre Museum, Paris, France. Licensed under CC by 2.0.

Page 94-95, 99, 101, Juan Alonso Rodriquez, JuanAlonsoStudio.com, used with permission.

Page 103, top left, Kseniya Sovenko; Top right, Armin Pressler; middle left, Clare Lighton; middle right, Jaya King; bottom left Robert Jean Ray. All used with permission.

Page 105, Patrice Drago, used with permission.

<h1 style="text-align:center">RESOURCES</h1>

Websites:

AcrylicDiva.com - My online and studio teaching site including general art sales.

Learn.AcrylicDiva.com - My online school.

BlackburnFineArt.com - My fine art portfolio and commissions site including commercial inquiries.

GoldenPaints.com. - My preferred brand of acrylic paint.

ArtsandCulture.google.com. - Google Arts and Culture Project.

MetMuseum.org/toah. - Heilbrunn Timeline of Art History.

Commons.Wikimedia.org. - Open source media.

Bibliography:

Gilbert, Elizabeth. Big Magic: Creative Living Beyond Fear. Riverhead Publishers, 2015.

Kandinsky, Wassily. Concerning the Spiritual in Art. Dover Publications; revised edition, June 1997.

Pressfield, Steven. The War of Art. Black Irish Books. November 2011.

Further Reading:

Baxandall Michael. Painting and Experience in Fifteenth-Century Italy: A Primer in the Social History of Pictorial Style (Oxford Paperbacks). July 1988.

Hughes, Robert. Shock of the New. Alfred A. Knopf. 1981.

Kleon, Austin. Steal Like an Artist. Workman Publishing. February 2012.

Kleon, Austin. Show Your Work: Ten Ways to Share Your Creativity and Get Discovered. Workman Publishing. March 2014.

Pressfield, Steven. Do The Work. The Domino Project/Black Irish Entertainment. September 2014.

Pressfield, Steven. Turning Pro. Black Irish Books. May 2012.

Tharp, Twyla. The Creative Habit: Learn It and Use It for Life. Simon and Schuster. March 2009.

Vasari, Giorgio. The Lives of the Artists (Oxford World Classics). April 1998.

Index

U

ugly 68
Union Square 90
Updike, John 83
UVLS polymer varnish 99

V

van Gogh, Vincent 20, 38, 46, 54, 82, 104
Vermeer 81
Voltaire 40
Vonnegut, Kurt 19
voodoo 76

W

Warhol, Andy 64
War of Art, The 35
Williams Sonoma 24
woo-woo 67
Wyeth, Andrew 57

Y

youngster 22

Z

Zola, Emile 99